Whisper Wild: Discovering Nature's Unspoken Language

Table of Contents

Introduction 5
   Purpose of the Book 5
   The Fascination with Hidden Messages 9
   How Nature Holds Clues 12
Understanding Symbolism in Nature 16
   Symbolism and its Significance 16
   Cultural Interpretations of Natural Symbols 19
   The Language of Animals and Plants 22
The Art of Observation 27
   Developing the Observational Skills 27
   Noticing Patterns and Anomalies 30
   Connecting the Dots 33

- The Hidden Codes of Colors.............................37
  - The Psychology of Colors in Nature 37
  - Color Symbolism in Different Cultures..........40
  - Decoding Colors in Animals and Plants........44
- Shapes and Structures as Messages 48
  - Geometric Patterns in Nature......................48
  - Sacred Geometry and its Role in Natural Forms 51
  - Architecture of Nests, Hives, and Burrows ..55
- Animal Behavior and Communication 59
  - Understanding Animal Communication.......59
  - Vocalizations, Body Language, and Gestures 62
  - Social Hierarchies and Mating Rituals..........66
- Hidden Messages in Landscapes......................71
  - Natural Landforms as Symbols 71
  - Ancient Petroglyphs and Their Meaning......74
  - The Art of Geomancy 77
- Unveiling Secrets through Nature's Cycles 82
  - The Symbolism of Seasons...........................82
  - Lunar and Solar Cycles 85
  - Animal Migration and Seasonal Patterns.....88

Hidden Messages in Plants and Flowers..........93

    The Language of Flowers 93

    Medicinal and Symbolic Properties of Plants 96

    Plant Communication and Defense Mechanisms...99

The Enigma of Symbiotic Relationships 104

    Mutualism, Commensalism, and Parasitism 104

    Decoding Hidden Messages in Interactions 107

    The Role of Symbiosis in Ecosystems.........111

Deciphering Weather Patterns 115

    Weather as a Language...............................115

    Reading Cloud Formations..........................117

    Animal and Plant Behavior as Weather Indicators 120

Enhancing Your Nature Connection...............123

    Cultivating Mindfulness in Nature 123

    Nature Meditation and Deepening Awareness 126

    Nature Rituals and Celebrations.................129

Ethical Considerations in Nature Interpretation 133

Respecting Wildlife and Habitats 133

Responsible Nature Photography and Documenting 136

Balancing Interpretation and Preservation 139

Conclusion 144

Continuing the Journey of Discovery 144

Embracing Nature's Hidden Messages 147

Introduction

Purpose of the Book

The purpose of this book is to unveil the captivating realm of hidden messages within nature. Nature has long been a source of inspiration and wonder for humanity, but beneath its surface lies a treasure trove of symbols, codes, and messages waiting to be discovered. This book seeks to awaken the reader's curiosity and deepen their connection with the natural world by revealing the secrets that nature holds.

In our modern society, we often find ourselves detached from the rhythms and subtleties of the natural world. We rush through life, oblivious to the intricate patterns and messages encoded in every leaf, rock, and creature that surrounds us. This book aims to bridge that gap and reignite our sense of awe and curiosity about nature's hidden language.

By exploring the symbolism found in nature, we can gain a profound understanding of the world around us. Symbols have played a crucial role in human culture for centuries, and the natural world is teeming with its own set of symbols, often carrying universal meaning and significance. Understanding these symbols unlocks a deeper level of interpretation and appreciation for the natural wonders we encounter every day.

Furthermore, this book delves into the cultural interpretations of natural symbols, recognizing that different societies and traditions assign unique meanings to various elements of nature. By examining these diverse perspectives, we can broaden our own understanding and appreciation of the interconnectedness between nature and human culture.

Central to this exploration is the concept of observation. The art of observation lies at the heart of deciphering nature's hidden messages. By cultivating our observational skills, we can learn to notice patterns, anomalies, and connections that are easily overlooked. This heightened awareness allows us to perceive the subtle messages embedded within nature's tapestry.

One fascinating aspect explored in this book is the hidden codes of colors. Colors have the power to evoke emotions and convey messages, and the natural world is rich with an array of vibrant hues. By understanding the psychology of colors in nature and the cultural symbolism attached to them, we can unlock a deeper layer of meaning hidden within animals, plants, and landscapes.

Shapes and structures also hold messages in nature. Geometric patterns, sacred geometry, and the architecture of nests, hives, and burrows all offer insights into the language of nature. By recognizing these patterns and understanding their significance, we can decipher the messages embedded in the very structures that animals and plants create.

Animal behavior and communication are another key area of exploration in this book. Animals have their own intricate systems of communication, employing vocalizations, body language, and gestures to convey messages within their species. By unraveling the secrets of animal communication, we gain a glimpse into their social hierarchies, mating rituals, and survival strategies.

Furthermore, this book delves into the hidden messages present in landscapes. Natural landforms often carry symbolic meanings, and ancient petroglyphs provide glimpses into the cultural interpretations of these symbols. Additionally, the practice of geomancy, the art of divination through interpreting the earth's energy, offers yet another lens through which we can understand the hidden messages within landscapes.

Nature's cycles provide yet another avenue for exploration. The symbolism of seasons, the dance of lunar and solar cycles, and the patterns of animal migration all reveal hidden messages about the ebb and flow of life. By deciphering these cycles, we can gain a deeper appreciation for the interconnectedness of all living beings.

Plants and flowers, too, have their own language. The study of the language of flowers unveils a world of symbolism and meaning, while the medicinal and symbolic properties of plants offer insights into their hidden messages. Moreover, plants communicate with each other and employ defense mechanisms in ways that often go unnoticed. Understanding these messages enriches our understanding of the plant kingdom.

The enigmatic world of symbiotic relationships holds its own hidden messages. The delicate balance of mutualism, commensalism, and parasitism within ecosystems carries deeper meanings. By decoding the hidden messages within these interactions, we gain a profound understanding of the intricate web of life.

Weather patterns also hold clues and messages. Weather itself can be seen as a language, and by learning to read cloud formations and observing the behavior of animals and plants in response to weather, we can uncover a new layer of understanding in our environment.

Lastly, this book draws upon the wisdom of ancient traditions. Indigenous knowledge systems, shamanism, mythology, and folklore have long recognized the hidden messages within nature. By exploring these rich traditions, we gain insights and guidance on our own journey of discovery.

In essence, the purpose of this book is to awaken a sense of wonder, curiosity, and connection with nature. By unveiling the hidden messages within the natural world, we hope to inspire readers to explore, observe, and embrace the beauty and wisdom that surrounds us. May this journey deepen your appreciation for nature's language and ignite a lifelong pursuit of discovering its hidden secrets.

The Fascination with Hidden Messages

There is an innate fascination within human beings when it comes to hidden messages. We are drawn to the idea that there is more beneath the surface, that there are deeper meanings waiting to be discovered. This fascination extends beyond the realms of human creation and reaches into the natural world that surrounds us.

Nature, with its abundant beauty and intricate complexities, captivates our imagination and stirs our curiosity. We look at a forest and see more than just trees; we see a tapestry of hidden messages woven into the landscape. We observe animals and plants and wonder about the secrets they hold, the stories they tell through their behavior and appearance.

Perhaps this fascination with hidden messages stems from our own desire for connection and meaning. We seek to find our place in the grand scheme of things, to unravel the mysteries that lie beyond the surface of our existence. And nature, with its vast array of symbols, codes, and messages, offers a doorway to unlock these deeper truths.

Hidden messages in nature speak to our sense of wonder and awe. They remind us that there is more to life than what meets the eye, that there is a profound interconnectedness between all living beings. By unraveling these messages, we tap into a universal language that transcends cultural boundaries and speaks directly to our souls.

The allure of hidden messages in nature lies in the sense of discovery and revelation they bring. It is the thrill of stumbling upon a symbol or deciphering a code that has been present all along, yet unnoticed. It is the satisfaction of connecting the dots, of piecing together the fragments to reveal a larger, more profound picture.

Hidden messages in nature also hold a sense of wisdom and guidance. They offer insights into the cycles of life, the interconnectedness of ecosystems, and the delicate balance that sustains our planet. By understanding these messages, we gain a deeper appreciation for the intricate dance of nature and our role within it.

Furthermore, hidden messages in nature spark our imagination and inspire creativity. They invite us to interpret and engage with the world in new and unexpected ways. As we explore the symbolism, colors, shapes, and behaviors found in nature, we tap into a wellspring of inspiration that can fuel artistic expression, scientific inquiry, and spiritual growth.

In a world that often feels disconnected and fragmented, the fascination with hidden messages in nature provides a sense of unity and purpose. It reminds us that we are part of a larger tapestry, that there are mysteries waiting to be unraveled, and that our existence is intertwined with the natural world.

The fascination with hidden messages in nature beckons us to explore, observe, and embrace the beauty and wisdom that surround us. It invites us to venture beyond the surface and dive into the depths of nature's language. May we embark on this journey with open hearts and minds, ready to discover the hidden messages that nature lovingly whispers to us.

How Nature Holds Clues

Nature, with its intricate patterns, rhythms, and interconnections, holds a wealth of clues that invite us to explore and decipher its hidden messages. It is a vast tapestry woven with symbols, colors, shapes, and behaviors, each carrying profound meaning and significance. By attuning ourselves to these clues, we unlock a deeper understanding of the natural world and our place within it.

One of the ways nature holds clues is through its symbolism. Symbols are like signposts, guiding us to deeper layers of interpretation and understanding. From the majestic eagle representing freedom and vision to the delicate lotus flower symbolizing purity and spiritual awakening, nature's symbols resonate across cultures and time, transcending language barriers. They invite us to contemplate the universal truths and archetypal meanings that they embody.

Colors, too, play a significant role in nature's clues. Each color carries its own energy and symbolism, evoking emotions and conveying messages. The vibrant red of a ripe apple signals vitality and passion, while the soothing blue of a clear sky speaks of tranquility and expansiveness. By observing the colors present in the natural world, we can decode the messages they communicate and gain a deeper appreciation for the richness and diversity of life.

Nature also speaks to us through shapes and structures. The intricate symmetry of a snowflake, the spirals of a seashell, and the fractal patterns in a leaf—all reveal the underlying principles of sacred geometry that permeate the natural world. These shapes hold inherent meaning and convey messages of harmony, balance, and growth. By recognizing and interpreting these shapes, we glimpse the hidden order that underlies the apparent chaos of nature.

Behaviors exhibited by animals and plants offer yet another avenue through which nature holds clues. From the intricate dances of courtship rituals to the communal cooperation within an ant colony, the behaviors of living beings carry messages about social structures, survival strategies, and the interconnectedness of species. By observing and deciphering these behaviors, we gain insights into the intricacies of nature's tapestry.

Furthermore, nature's clues can be found in the landscapes that surround us. The rugged peaks of mountains, the meandering flow of rivers, and the gentle undulations of sand dunes—they all tell stories of geological forces, climatic changes, and the passage of time. These landscapes carry messages about the Earth's history, the shaping of ecosystems, and the profound forces at work in shaping our planet. By attuning ourselves to the messages embedded within landscapes, we develop a deeper connection to the land and its stories.

Cycles and rhythms found in nature provide yet another layer of clues. The changing of seasons, the waxing and waning of the moon, and the ebb and flow of tides—all reveal the cyclical nature of life. These cycles hold messages about renewal, transformation, and the interconnectedness of all living things. By aligning ourselves with these natural rhythms, we harmonize with the flow of life and gain a deeper understanding of our own existence.

Nature's clues can also be found in the intricate communication systems employed by animals and plants. From the melodious songs of birds to the chemical signals released by plants, the natural world is alive with messages that facilitate survival, reproduction, and cooperation. By listening and observing these forms of communication, we tap into the intricate web of relationships and interconnectedness that define ecosystems.

Nature holds clues that invite us to embark on a journey of discovery and connection. By attuning ourselves to the symbolism, colors, shapes, behaviors, landscapes, cycles, and communication systems present in nature, we uncover a vast treasure trove of wisdom, beauty, and meaning. Nature becomes our teacher, guiding us to a deeper understanding of ourselves, the natural world, and the intricate tapestry of life.

Understanding Symbolism in Nature

Symbolism and its Significance

Symbolism is a powerful language that transcends words and speaks directly to our intuition and emotions. In the realm of nature, symbolism holds a profound significance, revealing hidden messages that invite us to delve deeper into the mysteries of the natural world.

Nature is replete with symbols, each carrying its own unique meaning and representing concepts that resonate across cultures and time. These symbols connect us to something larger than ourselves, bridging the gap between the tangible and the intangible. They invite us to contemplate the deeper truths that lie beneath the surface of our existence.

One of the significant aspects of symbolism in nature is its universality. Many symbols found in nature hold similar meanings across different cultures and civilizations. The sun, for instance, is often associated with warmth, vitality, and enlightenment, regardless of cultural background. This universality speaks to the deep-rooted connections we share as human beings, as we find common threads in our interpretations of nature's symbols.

The significance of symbolism in nature lies in its ability to transcend language barriers. Unlike spoken or written language, symbols communicate directly to our subconscious mind, bypassing the need for translation or interpretation. They tap into our primal instincts, evoking emotions and stirring a sense of wonder and awe. Symbols allow us to communicate and understand on a deeper, more intuitive level.

Symbols found in nature often reflect archetypal themes and universal concepts. The tree, with its roots firmly planted in the earth and branches reaching towards the sky, symbolizes growth, connection, and spiritual ascent. The circle, symbolizing wholeness and unity, can be seen in the cycles of life, from the rising and setting of the sun to the perpetual motion of the seasons. These archetypal symbols connect us to timeless wisdom and invite us to contemplate the larger tapestry of existence.

Moreover, symbolism in nature serves as a gateway to the sacred. Many ancient cultures and spiritual traditions revered nature as a source of divine wisdom and guidance. They recognized that symbols found in the natural world were imbued with sacred energy and carried messages from the spiritual realms. By attuning ourselves to these symbols, we open ourselves to the possibility of spiritual awakening and deeper connection with the divine.

The significance of symbolism in nature extends beyond the individual level. It speaks to the interconnectedness of all living beings and the web of life that binds us together. Animals, plants, and landscapes each have their own symbolic language, contributing to the larger narrative of the natural world. By understanding and interpreting these symbols, we gain insights into the delicate balance of ecosystems, the interdependence of species, and the intricate dance of life.

Furthermore, symbolism in nature offers a sense of guidance and meaning in our own lives. When we encounter a symbol in nature—a butterfly, a thunderstorm, or a blooming flower—it can act as a signpost, reminding us of certain qualities, lessons, or energies that we need to embody or explore. These symbols guide us on our personal journeys, offering support, inspiration, and deeper understanding.

Symbolism in nature holds immense significance and invites us to embark on a journey of exploration and interpretation. It connects us to the timeless wisdom of the natural world, transcending language barriers and evoking a sense of wonder and connection. By embracing and understanding the symbolism in nature, we gain insights into ourselves, the world around us, and the profound mysteries that lie within.

Cultural Interpretations of Natural Symbols

The interpretation of natural symbols is deeply intertwined with cultural beliefs, traditions, and folklore. Different cultures throughout history have ascribed unique meanings and interpretations to the symbols found in nature, reflecting their worldview, values, and spiritual practices. Exploring these cultural interpretations allows us to expand our understanding of the hidden messages within the natural world.

In many indigenous cultures, nature is seen as a sacred realm filled with spiritual significance. Symbols found in nature hold profound meaning, representing cosmic forces, deities, or ancestral spirits. For example, the snake is often revered as a symbol of transformation and rebirth in various indigenous traditions, representing the shedding of old layers to embrace new beginnings. The eagle, with its ability to soar to great heights, is associated with divine messages and spiritual guidance.

In Eastern philosophies, such as Buddhism and Taoism, nature is seen as an expression of the divine and a reflection of universal principles. Symbolism in nature is deeply rooted in these philosophies, reflecting concepts like balance, harmony, and the interplay of opposites. The yin-yang symbol, with its black and white halves, represents the dualistic forces of nature, signifying the interconnectedness and interdependence of all things.

In Western cultures, symbolism in nature has often been influenced by mythology, folklore, and religious traditions. For instance, the oak tree holds significance in Celtic mythology, symbolizing strength, wisdom, and longevity. In Christian symbolism, the lamb represents purity and sacrifice, while the dove is associated with peace and the Holy Spirit. These cultural interpretations enrich our understanding of the natural symbols, adding layers of meaning that have been passed down through generations.

The interpretation of natural symbols can also vary within cultural contexts. Different regions or subcultures may assign distinct meanings to the same symbol based on their unique experiences and local environments. For instance, the lotus flower, while universally associated with purity and spiritual awakening, may hold additional connotations in specific cultural contexts. In ancient Egypt, the lotus symbolized rebirth and the sun, while in Hinduism, it represented divine beauty and enlightenment.

Cultural interpretations of natural symbols not only provide insights into specific belief systems but also foster a deeper connection with the natural world. They encourage us to view nature through different lenses, expanding our perspectives and nurturing a greater appreciation for the diversity of symbolic languages that exist.

It is important to approach cultural interpretations with respect and an open mind, recognizing the richness and complexity of each tradition. By studying and appreciating these cultural interpretations, we gain a broader understanding of the intricate relationships between humans and nature, as well as the diverse ways in which people find meaning and guidance in the natural world.

Exploring cultural interpretations of natural symbols invites us to reflect on our own cultural backgrounds and personal experiences. It encourages us to examine the symbols and beliefs that have shaped our worldview and to question the meanings we ascribe to nature's signs and messages. By engaging in this exploration, we deepen our connection with our own cultural heritage while also embracing the universal language of nature's symbols.

Cultural interpretations of natural symbols provide a rich tapestry of meanings and perspectives. They illuminate the diverse ways in which different cultures have engaged with and understood the natural world. By appreciating and studying these interpretations, we broaden our understanding of the hidden messages within nature and foster a greater sense of interconnectedness with cultures around the globe.

The Language of Animals and Plants

Animals and plants possess a remarkable language of their own, a subtle and intricate form of communication that reveals a wealth of hidden messages. By observing and decoding the language of animals and plants, we gain a deeper understanding of their behaviors, needs, and the complex interconnectedness of the natural world.

Animals employ a variety of methods to communicate with one another, each tailored to their specific species and social structures. Vocalizations, such as the haunting songs of whales or the melodic chirping of birds, carry messages of warning, courtship, and territorial boundaries. These sounds convey emotions and intentions, allowing individuals within a species to establish social hierarchies, form bonds, and coordinate group activities.

But animal communication extends beyond vocalizations. Body language plays a crucial role in conveying messages. A raised tail or arched back in a cat signifies aggression or fear, while a wagging tail in a dog expresses excitement or friendliness. The flapping of wings or the display of colorful plumage in birds communicate mating availability or territorial defense. Animals utilize a vast array of physical cues, gestures, and postures to convey their intentions and emotions, creating a silent but potent language of their own.

Interestingly, some animals employ chemical signals as a means of communication. Pheromones, for example, are chemical substances released by an animal to convey information to others of its species. They can be used to mark territories, attract mates, or warn of danger. Ants utilize pheromones to create complex trails that guide their fellow colony members to food sources. In the natural world, these chemical messages shape behavior, promote cooperation, and ensure the survival and success of the species.

Plants, too, possess their own language, albeit one that is more subtle and less easily discernible to human perception. Through chemical signals and physical adaptations, plants communicate with their environment and other organisms. When under attack by herbivores, for instance, some plants release chemical signals that attract predators or release toxins to deter the attackers. In symbiotic relationships, plants communicate with beneficial organisms such as pollinators, offering nectar or producing specific scents to attract them.

Root systems also serve as a conduit for plant communication. Through underground networks, plants can transmit chemical signals and exchange vital nutrients or warnings with neighboring plants. This hidden language allows plants to respond collectively to environmental cues and ensure the survival of the community as a whole.

Furthermore, plants communicate with the world through their physical characteristics. The color and scent of flowers, for example, serve as invitations to pollinators, guiding them towards the reproductive organs of the plant. The shapes and textures of leaves may reflect adaptations to environmental conditions, allowing the plant to maximize light exposure or conserve water.

By deciphering the language of animals and plants, we gain a deeper appreciation for the intricacies of the natural world. We begin to understand the web of interdependence and the delicate balance that exists among species. Moreover, we learn to recognize the ways in which our own actions and choices impact the lives of other organisms.

Studying the language of animals and plants requires patience, keen observation, and an open mind. It necessitates attuning ourselves to the subtleties of the natural world, listening to the whispers of the wind, the rustling of leaves, and the calls of distant creatures. By immersing ourselves in their language, we develop a profound respect for the wisdom and interconnectedness that permeate the natural world.

In conclusion, the language of animals and plants is a fascinating realm that reveals hidden messages and insights into the intricate tapestry of life. By decoding their vocalizations, body language, chemical signals, and physical adaptations, we deepen our understanding of their behaviors, needs, and the complex relationships that sustain ecosystems. Through this exploration, we cultivate a sense of wonder and reverence for the diverse languages that exist within the natural world.

The Art of Observation

Developing the Observational Skills

In our fast-paced and modern world, it's easy to become disconnected from the intricate details and hidden messages that nature holds. However, by honing our observational skills, we can unlock a world of hidden wonders and embark on a journey of discovery.

Observation is more than just seeing; it's about paying attention to the intricate details, patterns, and nuances that exist in the natural world. It requires us to slow down, be present, and engage all our senses in the act of perceiving.

One of the fundamental aspects of developing observational skills is cultivating a state of mindfulness. By quieting our minds and fully immersing ourselves in the present moment, we become receptive to the subtleties of nature. We notice the delicate dance of sunlight filtering through the leaves, the gentle sway of grass in the breeze, or the intricate patterns on a butterfly's wings. Mindfulness allows us to be fully present in the natural world and heightens our ability to observe and appreciate its hidden messages.

Another important aspect of observation is developing a keen eye for detail. It involves training ourselves to notice the small and often overlooked elements that contribute to the larger tapestry of nature. It's about noticing the intricate patterns on a flower petal, the tracks left by animals in the mud, or the subtle changes in color that signal the changing of seasons. By actively seeking out and appreciating these details, we enhance our ability to decipher the hidden messages that nature presents.

Observation also entails patience and perseverance. Nature unfolds at its own pace, and many of its wonders reveal themselves only to those who are willing to invest time and effort. By spending dedicated moments in nature, we become attuned to its rhythms and patterns. We notice the repeated behaviors of animals, the cyclical changes in vegetation, and the subtle shifts in weather. Through patient observation, we unlock a deeper understanding of the intricate interconnectedness of the natural world.

Developing observational skills also involves engaging all our senses. While sight is often our primary sense for observation, we should not neglect the valuable information that our other senses provide. The fragrance of flowers, the sound of birdsong, the feel of tree bark—all these sensory inputs contribute to a richer and more holistic understanding of the natural environment. By engaging all our senses, we create a multi-dimensional experience that brings us closer to the hidden messages of nature.

In today's technology-driven world, it's important to recognize the impact of distractions on our ability to observe. The constant presence of screens and electronic devices can hinder our capacity to truly immerse ourselves in the natural world. Therefore, developing observational skills requires us to disconnect from technology and create space for uninterrupted and focused observation. By doing so, we open ourselves up to a deeper connection with nature and the hidden messages it offers.

Developing observational skills is a lifelong journey. It's not a destination but a continuous process of growth and refinement. Each encounter with nature presents new opportunities for observation and discovery. The more we practice, the more attuned we become to the subtleties and hidden messages that nature presents.

Developing observational skills is a transformative journey that allows us to unlock the hidden wonders of nature. By cultivating mindfulness, keen attention to detail, patience, and engagement of all our senses, we enhance our ability to perceive and interpret the messages that nature offers. It is through this deep observation that we foster a profound connection with the natural world and embark on a lifelong adventure of exploration and discovery.

Noticing Patterns and Anomalies

In the intricate tapestry of nature, patterns and anomalies abound, offering a wealth of hidden messages waiting to be deciphered. By training ourselves to notice these patterns and anomalies, we gain valuable insights into the workings of the natural world and tap into its underlying wisdom.

Patterns are the threads that weave together the fabric of nature. They can be found at various scales, from the microscopic to the grandest landscapes. From the delicate spirals of a seashell to the intricate fractal patterns in a snowflake, nature is replete with recurring motifs. These patterns often reflect fundamental principles of organization, efficiency, and growth.

By cultivating our ability to notice patterns, we uncover the hidden order that underlies seemingly chaotic natural phenomena. We may observe the rhythmic ebb and flow of tides, the repeated symmetry of flower petals, or the precise formations of migrating flocks of birds. Patterns offer insights into the fundamental processes and relationships that shape the natural world.

Anomalies, on the other hand, are deviations from established patterns. They are the unexpected and unique occurrences that catch our attention and invite further exploration. Anomalies challenge our preconceived notions and open doors to new understanding. They can be disruptions in the expected behaviors of animals, unusual colorations or markings in plants, or unexpected geological formations.

Noticing anomalies requires us to be open-minded and receptive to the unexpected. It is in these deviations from the norm that hidden messages often lie. Anomalies may signal environmental changes, evolutionary adaptations, or even undiscovered phenomena. By paying attention to these deviations, we gain a deeper appreciation for the complexity and resilience of the natural world.

Noticing patterns and anomalies goes beyond mere observation; it requires a curious and inquisitive mindset. It is about asking questions and seeking connections. Why do certain plants bloom in synchrony? What causes the variations in plumage among birds of the same species? How do anomalies contribute to the overall balance of ecosystems? By delving deeper into these questions, we embark on a journey of discovery and unravel the hidden messages that nature presents.

The ability to notice patterns and anomalies also extends beyond the boundaries of individual species or ecosystems. It allows us to perceive larger-scale phenomena and recognize the interconnectedness of nature on a global scale. By noticing patterns in weather systems, for example, we can anticipate seasonal changes and predict the behavior of migrating animals. By observing anomalies in climate patterns, we gain insights into the impact of human activities on the environment.

Noticing patterns and anomalies requires practice and a heightened level of awareness. It necessitates a shift in perspective, encouraging us to view nature as a dynamic and interconnected system. It is not a passive act but an active engagement with the natural world, where we become detectives unraveling the secrets that nature presents.

Developing the skill of noticing patterns and anomalies is a gateway to unlocking the hidden messages in nature. By recognizing recurring motifs and unexpected deviations, we gain insights into the fundamental workings of the natural world. This skill fosters a sense of curiosity and wonder, inviting us to explore the interconnectedness of species, ecosystems, and global phenomena. Through the lens of patterns and anomalies, we embark on a continuous journey of discovery, deepening our understanding of the profound mysteries that nature holds.

Connecting the Dots

In the intricate web of nature's tapestry, hidden messages are often scattered like puzzle pieces waiting to be connected. By cultivating the ability to connect the dots, we unveil a deeper understanding of the interrelationships and hidden meanings that permeate the natural world.

Connecting the dots involves recognizing and making sense of the myriad of observations, patterns, and anomalies we encounter. It is the art of weaving together diverse strands of information to form a cohesive and meaningful narrative. It requires us to approach nature with a holistic mindset, seeing beyond isolated events or individual species, and perceiving the larger interconnected web of life.

The process of connecting the dots begins with careful observation and data collection. We gather information from various sources—direct experiences, scientific studies, historical records, and indigenous knowledge. Each piece of information serves as a fragment of the puzzle, offering valuable insights into specific aspects of nature. We must be open to different perspectives and sources of knowledge, recognizing that the hidden messages of nature can be revealed through diverse lenses.

As we gather these puzzle pieces, we must resist the temptation to impose rigid frameworks or predetermined interpretations. Nature is a dynamic and complex system, constantly evolving and defying simplistic categorizations. Instead, we embrace a flexible and adaptive mindset, allowing the pieces to guide us towards their own natural connections.

Connecting the dots also requires us to transcend disciplinary boundaries. Nature is inherently interdisciplinary, with its phenomena spanning the realms of biology, ecology, geology, climatology, and more. By integrating knowledge from different disciplines, we gain a more comprehensive understanding of the hidden messages that nature presents. For example, understanding the relationship between weather patterns, plant phenology, and animal behavior can unveil intricate ecological dynamics.

Additionally, connecting the dots encourages us to explore the deep interdependencies between humans and the natural world. We recognize that our actions and choices have far-reaching consequences for the ecosystems we are a part of. By connecting the dots between human activities, environmental impacts, and the well-being of both natural and human communities, we gain a greater sense of responsibility and stewardship.

The process of connecting the dots is not always linear or straightforward. It requires patience, curiosity, and a willingness to embrace uncertainty. Sometimes, it is the unexpected connections that hold the greatest insights. By exploring seemingly unrelated phenomena or drawing parallels between disparate observations, we may stumble upon profound revelations that reshape our understanding of nature.

Furthermore, connecting the dots invites us to engage our intuition and embrace the wisdom of indigenous knowledge systems and traditional ecological practices. Indigenous cultures have long held deep connections with the natural world, recognizing its subtle messages and intricate relationships. By bridging traditional wisdom with scientific inquiry, we gain a more holistic and inclusive perspective, honoring the wisdom embedded in different ways of knowing.

Connecting the dots is a continuous and lifelong process. As we deepen our understanding of nature, new puzzle pieces emerge, and fresh connections present themselves. It is a journey of discovery, one that enriches our relationship with the natural world and fosters a sense of awe, wonder, and reverence.

Connecting the dots is a skill that allows us to unlock the hidden messages in nature and weave together a tapestry of understanding. It involves careful observation, integration of diverse knowledge, embracing interdisciplinary approaches, and recognizing the interconnectedness of all life. By connecting the dots, we embark on a transformative journey that deepens our appreciation for the complexity and beauty of the natural world.

The Hidden Codes of Colors

The Psychology of Colors in Nature

Colors are not merely visual phenomena; they possess a profound psychological impact that resonates within us at a deep level. In nature, colors play a significant role in conveying messages, eliciting emotions, and attracting attention. Understanding the psychology of colors allows us to decode the hidden messages embedded in nature's vibrant palette.

Color psychology explores the emotional and cognitive effects that different colors evoke in humans. While cultural and personal experiences can influence individual responses to colors, certain universal associations have been observed across cultures and contexts. Nature, with its diverse array of colors, harnesses these psychological influences to communicate and interact with its inhabitants.

Green, for instance, is a color often associated with nature and represents growth, vitality, and harmony. The lush green foliage of trees, the verdant meadows, and the vibrant mosses all evoke a sense of rejuvenation and tranquility. Research suggests that exposure to green environments can reduce stress levels, enhance mood, and foster a sense of well-being. In nature, green acts as a soothing balm, inviting us to connect with the vitality and balance inherent in the natural world.

Blue, with its calming and serene qualities, is often linked to water and the sky. The vast expanse of the ocean, the clear blue sky, and the delicate hue of a mountain lake evoke feelings of tranquility, peace, and expansiveness. Blue is known to promote relaxation, reduce anxiety, and enhance mental clarity. It invites us to contemplate the vastness and depth of nature's mysteries, encouraging introspection and a sense of connectedness.

Warm colors like red, orange, and yellow elicit feelings of energy, passion, and excitement. The fiery hues of a sunset, the vibrant petals of a flower, or the golden glow of sunlight evoke a sense of warmth and vitality. These colors can inspire action, creativity, and enthusiasm. They draw our attention, signaling importance, and stimulating our senses. In nature, warm colors act as invitations to engage, explore, and embrace the vitality of life.

White, often associated with purity and clarity, is found in the pristine snow-capped mountains, the delicate petals of white flowers, and the ethereal beauty of clouds. White signifies innocence, simplicity, and a sense of spaciousness. It evokes a feeling of purity and offers a clean slate for new beginnings. In nature, white carries a sense of stillness and purity, inviting us to appreciate the subtle details and find clarity amidst the noise of the world.

Black, though not strictly a color, is a presence of absence, symbolizing mystery, power, and depth. The dark night sky dotted with stars, the velvety petals of a black rose, or the shadowed depths of a dense forest evoke a sense of intrigue and the unknown. Black can be both comforting and unsettling, representing the hidden realms and the potential for transformation. In nature, black serves as a reminder that there are depths yet to be explored and secrets waiting to be revealed.

Nature's color palette is rich and varied, offering a tapestry of emotions and messages. By understanding the psychology of colors, we can decode the hidden meanings embedded in the natural world. We can attune ourselves to the emotions and sensations evoked by different colors, allowing us to deepen our connection with nature and enhance our appreciation of its hidden messages.

It is important to note that color symbolism can vary across cultures and individual interpretations. Cultural associations, personal experiences, and symbolic meanings attached to colors can shape our perception and response. Therefore, as we explore the psychology of colors in nature, we must remain open to the diverse interpretations and meanings that colors hold for different people and cultures.

The psychology of colors in nature offers a window into the hidden messages embedded in the natural world. Colors evoke emotions, convey meaning, and attract our attention. By paying attention to the psychological impact of colors, we can unravel the symbolism and significance that colors hold in nature. It is a journey of discovery that enhances our understanding, deepens our connection, and enriches our experience of the natural world.

Color Symbolism in Different Cultures

Colors have played a significant role in human cultures throughout history, serving as powerful symbols that communicate meaning, express emotions, and convey cultural values. The symbolism assigned to colors varies across different cultures, reflecting the unique perspectives and beliefs of each society. Exploring color symbolism in various cultures unveils a rich tapestry of interpretations and reveals how colors can carry profound messages in the natural world.

In Western cultures, for example, white is often associated with purity, innocence, and peace. It is the color of wedding gowns and is used to represent cleanliness and clarity. In contrast, black is often linked to mourning, death, and darkness. It carries a sense of mystery and elegance, but also signifies mourning and solemnity. Red, on the other hand, is frequently associated with passion, love, and vitality. It is a color that signifies energy and strength, and it is often used to evoke powerful emotions.

In Eastern cultures, such as China, colors hold specific symbolic meanings deeply rooted in ancient traditions. Red, for instance, is considered an auspicious color associated with luck, happiness, and celebration. It is often used in festive occasions, such as Chinese New Year, and is believed to bring good fortune. In India, red is also associated with vitality and fertility and is a significant color in wedding ceremonies. In Japan, red represents life force, energy, and courage.

The symbolism of other colors in Eastern cultures differs as well. In China, yellow holds great importance and is associated with royalty and power. It symbolizes the emperor and was traditionally reserved for imperial use. In Japan, yellow is linked to courage and bravery. Blue, in many Eastern cultures, represents spirituality and is associated with tranquility and calmness. It symbolizes the divine and is often used in religious art and architecture.

In indigenous cultures, color symbolism is deeply intertwined with the natural world and the spiritual beliefs of the community. Native American tribes, for instance, have distinct interpretations of colors based on their cultural heritage. White can represent purity and spirituality, while black can symbolize protection and transformation. The colors of the earth, such as brown and red, are often associated with grounding, connection to nature, and the cycles of life. Different tribes may have variations in their color symbolism, reflecting the unique perspectives and traditions of each community.

In African cultures, colors hold diverse meanings that vary across regions and tribes. For example, in many African societies, green symbolizes fertility, growth, and abundance. It represents the vitality of the land and the nourishment it provides. Red can signify life force, energy, and power, while also symbolizing danger or warning. Yellow is often associated with wealth, royalty, and prestige. Each color carries its own cultural significance, reflecting the diverse histories and beliefs of the African continent.

The study of color symbolism in different cultures highlights the profound ways in which colors can carry hidden messages and cultural significance. Understanding these symbolic associations enhances our ability to interpret and appreciate the messages nature communicates through its vibrant hues. It invites us to embrace the diversity of perspectives and interpretations, broadening our understanding of the interconnectedness between color, culture, and the natural world.

It is essential to approach color symbolism in different cultures with respect and cultural sensitivity. Colors can hold deep cultural, religious, and historical significance, and their interpretation may vary even within a single culture. It is crucial to engage in dialogue, learn from diverse cultural perspectives, and approach color symbolism with an open and curious mind.

Color symbolism in different cultures reveals the intricate and diverse ways in which colors are assigned meaning and significance. Exploring color symbolism allows us to appreciate the richness of cultural perspectives and deepens our understanding of the hidden messages conveyed through nature's vibrant palette. By embracing the cultural diversity of color symbolism, we can expand our awareness, foster cross-cultural understanding, and celebrate the multifaceted beauty of the natural world

Decoding Colors in Animals and Plants

In the natural world, colors are not exclusive to human experiences; they permeate the lives of animals and plants as well. Just as colors hold symbolic meanings for humans, they also play a vital role in the communication, survival, and reproduction of various species. Decoding the colors exhibited by animals and plants unveils a fascinating realm of hidden messages and adaptations that shape their interactions with the environment and other organisms.

In the animal kingdom, colors serve multiple purposes. For some species, vibrant and conspicuous colors act as signals, communicating crucial information to potential mates or rivals. Male birds, for example, often display colorful plumage during the breeding season to attract females and establish dominance over competitors. The bright red feathers of a male cardinal or the iridescent blues and greens of a peacock are visual cues that convey genetic fitness and reproductive prowess.

Color patterns in animals can also serve as camouflage or warning signals. Many insects, such as butterflies and beetles, have evolved intricate patterns that mimic their surroundings, making them difficult for predators to detect. This camouflage allows them to blend seamlessly into their environments, increasing their chances of survival. Conversely, some animals display vibrant colors as a warning to potential predators, indicating toxicity or danger. The vibrant red and black markings of a ladybug or the bold patterns of a venomous snake communicate the potential risks associated with approaching or attacking them.

Plants, too, employ colors as a means of communication and adaptation. Flowers, in particular, have evolved an astonishing array of colors to attract pollinators and ensure successful reproduction. Each flower color appeals to specific pollinators, such as bees, butterflies, or birds, that are attracted to particular wavelengths of light. For instance, bees are drawn to yellow and blue flowers, while hummingbirds are more attracted to red and orange hues. The colors serve as beacons, guiding pollinators to the nectar-rich rewards within the flowers and facilitating the crucial process of pollination.

Beyond pollination, colors in plants can also signify ripeness, warning of toxicity, or act as protective mechanisms. Fruits often change color as they ripen, signaling their readiness for consumption and seed dispersal. The vibrant hues of ripe berries or the golden tones of a mature ear of corn entice animals to consume them, aiding in seed dispersal. In contrast, some plants exhibit warning colors, such as the bright red or orange of poisonous mushrooms or berries, deterring animals from consuming them due to their toxic properties.

Moreover, colors in plants can serve as protective adaptations. The green pigment chlorophyll, responsible for the color of most leaves, plays a crucial role in photosynthesis, allowing plants to convert sunlight into energy. This green coloration not only enables plants to capture essential light energy but also provides them with camouflage in a foliage-rich environment, helping them blend in with their surroundings and avoid detection by herbivores.

Decoding colors in animals and plants requires an understanding of the specific ecological contexts and evolutionary adaptations of each species. It involves unraveling the intricate interplay between genetic traits, environmental factors, and the selective pressures that have shaped the colors we observe in nature. It is a fascinating journey of discovery that enhances our appreciation of the complexity and beauty of the natural world.

Studying the colors exhibited by animals and plants can provide insights into the health of ecosystems and the impacts of environmental changes. Variations in coloration may indicate shifts in habitat quality, pollution levels, or the presence of disease. Monitoring and understanding these color signals can aid in conservation efforts, helping to protect and restore the delicate balance of ecosystems.

Decoding the colors displayed by animals and plants unravels a captivating world of hidden messages, adaptations, and ecological dynamics. Colors serve as signals, camouflage, warnings, and reproductive cues, allowing organisms to communicate, survive, and thrive in their respective environments. By delving into the fascinating realm of color in nature, we gain a deeper understanding of the intricate relationships between species and their surroundings, and we unlock the profound significance of colors as a universal language that connects us to the hidden wonders of the natural world.

Shapes and Structures as Messages

Geometric Patterns in Nature

Nature is a masterful artist, adorning the world with an array of mesmerizing geometric patterns that captivate our senses and spark our curiosity. From the intricate symmetry of snowflakes to the rhythmic spirals of seashells, geometric patterns abound in the natural realm, revealing the underlying order and beauty that permeates our universe. Exploring the significance and origins of these patterns allows us to unravel hidden messages and gain a deeper appreciation for the interconnectedness of all living things.

One of the most iconic geometric patterns found in nature is the spiral. It is a shape that manifests in various forms, from the delicate spiral of a seashell to the grand spiraling arms of galaxies. Spirals symbolize growth, expansion, and evolution. They reflect the Fibonacci sequence, a mathematical pattern in which each number is the sum of the two preceding numbers (0, 1, 1, 2, 3, 5, 8, etc.), often observed in the arrangement of leaves on a stem, the petals of a flower, or the scales on a pinecone. This sequence creates a visually harmonious spiral pattern that is found throughout nature, hinting at the underlying mathematical principles that govern the growth and organization of living organisms.

Fractals are another fascinating manifestation of geometric patterns in nature. A fractal is a complex pattern that repeats itself at different scales, revealing intricate detail and self-similarity. Examples of fractals can be seen in the branching patterns of trees, the intricate veins of leaves, or the delicate patterns found in snowflakes. These self-replicating patterns remind us of the interconnectedness of all things, as they emerge from simple rules and extend into the complexity of the natural world. Fractals symbolize the infinite possibilities and interconnected nature of existence, offering a glimpse into the profound unity that underlies the apparent diversity of life.

Hexagons are yet another geometric pattern prevalent in nature. Bees construct their hives in hexagonal cells, maximizing space efficiency while minimizing the use of resources. The hexagonal shape allows for a strong and stable structure, enabling bees to store honey and raise their young. Hexagons also appear in the delicate patterns of snowflakes, formed through the crystallization of water vapor. This geometric pattern represents efficiency, strength, and harmony, showcasing nature's innate wisdom in designing systems that are both functional and aesthetically pleasing.

The symmetry of shapes is another aspect of geometric patterns that fascinates and inspires. Symmetry can be observed in the bilateral symmetry of butterflies' wings, the radial symmetry of flowers, or the symmetrical patterns found in the scales of fish. Symmetry is visually appealing and is often associated with beauty and balance. It evokes a sense of order and harmony, reminding us of the intricate balance that exists in nature.

Geometric patterns in nature serve various purposes beyond their aesthetic appeal. They can assist in the functioning and survival of organisms. For example, the arrangement of leaves on a plant maximizes exposure to sunlight, allowing for efficient photosynthesis. The precise geometric patterns seen in the eyes of certain animals, such as the compound eyes of insects or the intricate patterns on butterfly wings, aid in vision and camouflage. These patterns help organisms navigate their environments, attract mates, or evade predators.

The study of geometric patterns in nature not only deepens our understanding of the natural world but also inspires human creativity and innovation. Many architects, designers, and artists draw inspiration from nature's geometric patterns, incorporating their beauty and efficiency into human-made structures and artworks. The exploration of geometric patterns in nature encourages us to seek harmony, balance, and sustainability in our own creations, mirroring the wisdom inherent in the natural world.

Geometric patterns in nature are a testament to the universal principles and mathematical order that shape our world. They embody beauty, efficiency, and interconnectedness, offering a glimpse into the profound mysteries of existence. By delving into the significance and origins of these patterns, we unlock hidden messages that connect us to the inherent wisdom and design of the natural world. Exploring and appreciating geometric patterns in nature enriches our lives and inspires us to seek harmony and balance in all aspects of our existence.

Sacred Geometry and its Role in Natural Forms

Throughout the ages, humans have recognized and revered the inherent beauty and profound significance of geometric patterns in the natural world. From ancient civilizations to modern thinkers, the concept of sacred geometry has captivated our imaginations, inviting us to explore the interconnectedness between mathematics, spirituality, and the mysteries of creation. Sacred geometry unveils the hidden messages encoded within the symmetrical and harmonious forms found in nature, offering insights into the divine order that permeates our existence.

At its core, sacred geometry is the study of geometric patterns and their symbolic meanings. It is a discipline that recognizes the inherent harmony, balance, and mathematical precision underlying the creation of the universe. These patterns can be observed in the structures of crystals, the branching of trees, the spirals of galaxies, and the intricate formations of flowers. They represent the fundamental building blocks of creation, revealing the interplay between the physical and the spiritual realms.

One of the most renowned geometric forms in sacred geometry is the golden ratio, also known as the divine proportion or Phi (ϕ). This ratio, approximately 1.618, is derived from a mathematical relationship in which the ratio of the whole to the larger part is the same as the ratio of the larger part to the smaller part. The golden ratio is found in various natural forms, such as the proportions of the human body, the growth patterns of plants, and the arrangement of petals in flowers like the sunflower or the rose. It is believed to evoke a sense of harmony, beauty, and perfection, resonating with the innate aesthetic preferences of the human mind.

Another significant geometric form in sacred geometry is the Vesica Piscis, a shape formed by the intersection of two overlapping circles. This symbol, resembling an almond shape or an eye, holds deep spiritual meaning and is considered a symbol of the divine feminine. It represents the union of opposites, the interplay between light and dark, and the creative energy that arises from their merging. The Vesica Piscis can be found in numerous natural forms, such as the eyes of certain animals, the patterns on fish scales, or the delicate petals of flowers. It serves as a reminder of the interconnectedness and unity of all things.

The flower of life is another sacred geometric pattern that has intrigued mystics and scholars for centuries. It is a symmetrical arrangement of overlapping circles, forming a complex and intricate lattice-like structure. This pattern can be found in ancient temples, art, and sacred sites around the world, suggesting its significance across diverse cultures and civilizations. The flower of life is believed to contain the blueprint of creation, representing the interconnectedness of all living beings and the underlying order that governs the universe. It symbolizes the interplay between the material and spiritual realms, reminding us of the eternal cycles of birth, growth, death, and rebirth.

Sacred geometry not only deepens our appreciation of the natural world but also serves as a spiritual tool for self-discovery and inner transformation. By meditating upon and contemplating these geometric forms, we align ourselves with the underlying patterns of creation, tapping into the universal wisdom and divine energy that permeates our existence. Sacred geometry can act as a bridge between the seen and the unseen, offering a pathway to explore the mysteries of consciousness and the interconnectedness of all beings.

Sacred geometry unveils the hidden wisdom and spiritual significance of geometric patterns in the natural world. It provides a framework for understanding the interconnectedness between mathematics, spirituality, and the mysteries of creation. By contemplating these sacred forms, we embark on a journey of self-discovery and connection with the divine. As we delve into the role of sacred geometry in natural forms, we deepen our understanding of the profound beauty and underlying order that shapes our universe.

Architecture of Nests, Hives, and Burrows

Nature is a master architect, and nowhere is this more evident than in the intricate and ingenious structures created by animals. Nests, hives, and burrows serve as not only shelters for these creatures but also as expressions of their innate intelligence and adaptive capabilities. By exploring the architecture of these remarkable constructions, we unravel the hidden messages embedded within, gaining insight into the complexity and harmony of the natural world.

Nests, constructed by a variety of bird species, are marvels of engineering. Each species displays its unique architectural style, carefully selecting materials and utilizing different construction techniques. Birds use a combination of twigs, leaves, mud, and other natural elements to build nests that provide protection, insulation, and support for their eggs and young. The shape and design of these nests are often tailored to the specific needs and behaviors of the species. Some birds create intricate woven structures, while others opt for simpler cup-shaped nests. The location of nests, whether hidden in trees, nestled in cliffs, or perched on branches, reflects a careful balance between protection and accessibility. The architecture of bird nests is a testament to the ingenuity and adaptability of these avian architects, and their construction techniques have inspired human architects and engineers throughout history.

Hives, the homes of social insects such as bees and wasps, exemplify the concept of collaborative architecture. Within a hive, thousands of individuals work together in perfect harmony to construct and maintain a complex structure. Bees, for example, build hexagonal cells using beeswax, a substance produced by their own bodies. The hexagonal shape maximizes space efficiency while providing strength and stability to the hive structure. The organization of cells within the hive is carefully planned, with different sections designated for brood rearing, honey storage, and pollen collection. The architecture of hives not only facilitates the survival and reproduction of the colony but also serves as a communication tool, allowing bees to convey important information through chemical signals and dance movements. The intricate design and cooperative efforts involved in building and maintaining hives demonstrate the remarkable abilities of these social insects and offer insights into the power of collaboration and division of labor.

Burrows, constructed by a range of animals including rodents, reptiles, and insects, provide essential shelter and protection. These underground structures vary in complexity and size, depending on the species and their specific needs. Burrows offer a safe haven from predators, extreme temperatures, and other environmental challenges. Animals such as rabbits, foxes, and prairie dogs dig intricate tunnel networks, complete with multiple chambers for different purposes. Burrows may include separate areas for nesting, storage, and even latrines. The architecture of burrows allows animals to create a secure and comfortable living space within the subterranean realm, where they can raise their young and seek refuge during adverse conditions. The construction of burrows demonstrates the resourcefulness and adaptability of these creatures, showcasing their ability to transform their surroundings into functional and protective habitats.

The architecture of nests, hives, and burrows not only serves practical purposes but also conveys messages about the behaviors, needs, and adaptations of the animals that construct them. These structures embody the innate wisdom and instincts of the species, reflecting their unique evolutionary histories and ecological relationships. They provide insight into the complex interplay between form and function, as well as the intricate balance between individual needs and the needs of the community. The study of nest-building, hive construction, and burrow excavation offers a glimpse into the remarkable diversity and ingenuity of life on Earth.

The architecture of nests, hives, and burrows is a testament to the creative intelligence and adaptive capabilities of animals. These structures showcase the remarkable abilities of creatures to design and construct living spaces that meet their specific needs. By delving into the hidden messages embedded within these architectural marvels, we gain a deeper appreciation for the intricacy and harmony of the natural world and the remarkable strategies employed by animals to thrive in their environments.

Animal Behavior and Communication

Understanding Animal Communication

Animals possess a rich and diverse repertoire of communication methods that allow them to convey information, establish social bonds, and navigate their environments. From complex vocalizations to subtle body language and chemical signals, the world of animal communication is a fascinating realm waiting to be explored. By delving into the intricacies of animal communication, we can unlock hidden messages and gain a deeper understanding of the behaviors and interactions of the creatures that share our planet.

Vocalizations play a prominent role in animal communication, serving as a means of conveying a wide range of messages. The melodic songs of birds are not merely expressions of beauty but also serve as signals to mark territories, attract mates, and communicate with their offspring. The variety and complexity of bird songs are astounding, with different species using distinct patterns and melodies to convey specific meanings. Similarly, mammals such as wolves, dolphins, and primates utilize vocalizations to communicate information about danger, group cohesion, and reproductive status. The intricate nuances of animal vocalizations reveal a sophisticated system of communication that extends far beyond mere sounds, conveying messages laden with meaning and intention.

Beyond vocalizations, animals employ a rich repertoire of body language to convey information and maintain social bonds. Postures, gestures, and facial expressions serve as nonverbal cues that communicate an array of messages. From the dominance displays of gorillas and the threat displays of reptiles to the elaborate courtship dances of birds, body language provides a visual language that allows animals to communicate their intentions, emotions, and social status. The subtle movements, displays of aggression, or displays of submission all play a vital role in establishing social hierarchies, resolving conflicts, and ensuring effective communication within a species.

Chemical signals are another fascinating aspect of animal communication. Pheromones, chemical compounds released into the environment, convey messages about reproductive status, territory marking, and social bonding. Insects, for example, use pheromones to attract mates, establish trail markers, and coordinate group activities. Similarly, mammals, including canines and felines, utilize scent marking as a means of communication, leaving olfactory messages to convey territorial boundaries, reproductive availability, and social affiliations. Chemical signals tap into a hidden realm of communication, imperceptible to the human senses but crucial for the animals that rely on them for navigation, reproduction, and survival.

Understanding animal communication goes beyond the study of individual signals and involves grasping the broader context in which these signals are exchanged. Animals possess intricate communication systems that incorporate a combination of vocalizations, body language, and chemical signals to convey complex messages. Context, including environmental cues, social dynamics, and individual experiences, influences the interpretation and reception of these signals. By studying the behavioral ecology of animals, we can unravel the hidden messages embedded within their communication systems, gaining insights into their social structures, reproductive strategies, and ecological adaptations.

The study of animal communication not only enriches our understanding of the natural world but also offers valuable insights into our own human communication systems. By examining the diverse ways in which animals convey information and establish social bonds, we gain a deeper appreciation for the complexity and universality of communication across species. We recognize that communication is not limited to verbal language but extends to a multitude of channels and modalities.

Animal communication is a fascinating field of study that unveils the hidden messages encoded within the vocalizations, body language, and chemical signals of animals. By exploring and understanding these communication systems, we gain a greater appreciation for the diversity and complexity of life on Earth. Animal communication serves as a reminder that beneath the surface of the natural world lies a vast web of interconnections, where messages are exchanged, social bonds are formed, and the intricate tapestry of life unfolds.

Vocalizations, Body Language, and Gestures

Communication in the natural world extends far beyond verbal language. Animals, insects, and other creatures possess a diverse range of vocalizations, body language, and gestures that enable them to convey messages, establish social bonds, and navigate their environments. By exploring the intricate world of nonverbal communication, we gain insight into the hidden messages encoded within these expressions, unraveling the complex tapestry of communication in the natural world.

Vocalizations are a primary means of communication for many animals. From the haunting calls of wolves to the melodious songs of birds, the animal kingdom is alive with a symphony of sounds. Each species has its unique vocal repertoire, utilizing a combination of tones, pitches, and rhythms to convey messages with precision. Birds use their songs to mark territories, attract mates, and communicate with their offspring. The intricate melodies and patterns of bird songs not only captivate our ears but also serve as a language through which they express their needs and emotions. Mammals, too, employ vocalizations to communicate, whether it be the roars of lions, the howls of wolves, or the complex vocalizations of primates. These sounds carry meaning, from expressing dominance and establishing boundaries to alerting others of danger or coordinating group activities.

Vocalizations provide a glimpse into the rich tapestry of animal communication, conveying messages that often transcend words.

But communication in the natural world is not limited to vocalizations alone. Body language and gestures play an integral role in conveying messages and establishing social bonds. Animals utilize a wide array of physical cues to communicate their intentions, emotions, and social status. From the gentle touch of a mother grooming her young to the dominant postures of animals asserting their authority, body language speaks volumes in the natural world. Postures, movements, and facial expressions carry nuanced meanings, allowing animals to convey their intentions and establish social hierarchies. The flaring of a peacock's feathers, the raised hackles of a dog, or the display of antlers by a deer are all visual signals that communicate a range of messages. Body language is a universal language in the animal kingdom, bridging the gap between different species and facilitating communication even in the absence of vocalizations.

Gestures, too, play a crucial role in communication among animals and insects. From intricate courtship dances to intricate mating displays, gestures are often elaborate and purposeful. Many birds engage in elaborate courtship rituals, involving synchronized movements, displays of plumage, and aerial acrobatics. These gestures are not only captivating to observe but also serve as powerful communication tools to attract mates and establish pair bonds. Insects, such as bees and ants, communicate through a complex system of chemical and tactile gestures. They utilize intricate movements and physical contact to convey information about food sources, danger, and the location of resources. These gestures are precise and intentional, ensuring effective communication within their colonies or communities.

Understanding the vocalizations, body language, and gestures of animals, insects, and other creatures allows us to decipher the hidden messages that permeate the natural world. It provides us with insights into their behaviors, social dynamics, and ecological adaptations. By studying and interpreting these nonverbal forms of communication, we gain a deeper appreciation for the complexity and richness of life on Earth. We recognize that communication in the natural world is a multifaceted tapestry of vocalizations, body language, and gestures, where messages are conveyed and received, social bonds are formed, and the survival of species is ensured.

The vocalizations, body language, and gestures of animals, insects, and other creatures in nature are a testament to the intricate communication systems that exist beyond verbal language. These nonverbal forms of communication convey messages, emotions, and intentions, enabling individuals within a species to interact, establish social bonds, and navigate their environments. Exploring and understanding these expressions deepens our connection with the natural world, unveiling the hidden messages encoded within the vibrant tapestry of communication that surrounds us.

Social Hierarchies and Mating Rituals

In the animal kingdom, social hierarchies and mating rituals are fascinating aspects of behavior that shape the dynamics within species and influence the selection of mates. These intricate systems of organization and courtship offer valuable insights into the hidden messages embedded within nature, revealing the strategies employed by individuals to ensure reproductive success and establish their place within the social fabric of their communities.

Social hierarchies are prevalent among various animal species, from mammals to birds and even insects. Within a social hierarchy, individuals occupy different ranks or positions based on factors such as dominance, aggression, or access to resources. Dominance hierarchies are especially common, with individuals vying for status and asserting their authority through displays of aggression, posturing, or other forms of social signaling. The establishment of a social hierarchy helps maintain order within a group, reducing conflict and facilitating cooperation. By understanding the subtle cues and behaviors associated with social hierarchies, we gain insight into the power dynamics and social structure of animal communities.

Mating rituals are another intriguing aspect of animal behavior, often characterized by elaborate displays, courtship dances, and intricate rituals aimed at attracting a mate. These rituals are vital in signaling reproductive fitness, compatibility, and genetic quality. Males often engage in extravagant displays of color, plumage, or physical prowess to capture the attention of females and outcompete rival suitors. Peacocks fan their vibrant tails, birds engage in synchronized aerial displays, and insects emit pheromones to entice potential mates. These rituals serve as a visual language, conveying messages about the health, strength, and suitability of individuals as potential partners.

Mating rituals are not limited to external displays alone but also involve behavioral interactions and communication between individuals. Birds may engage in elaborate courtship dances, where they perform intricate movements and vocalizations to impress potential mates. The synchronization of movements, the exchange of calls, and the coordination of displays all contribute to the complex communication that takes place during courtship. In some species, males offer gifts or engage in elaborate courtship rituals that demonstrate their commitment and suitability as partners. These rituals can be seen as a form of hidden communication, where individuals signal their qualities and intentions to potential mates.

The selection of a mate is a crucial decision for individuals in the animal kingdom, as it directly influences their reproductive success and the genetic diversity of the population. The process of mate selection often involves hidden messages embedded within the intricate displays and interactions of courtship. Females may assess the quality of males based on their displays, their ability to provide resources, or their overall fitness. In turn, males compete for the attention and favor of females, employing a range of strategies to enhance their chances of successful mating. These strategies may involve competition, cooperation, or even deception, as individuals strive to secure their place in the mating hierarchy and ensure the continuation of their genetic lineage.

Understanding social hierarchies and mating rituals provides us with a glimpse into the complex world of animal behavior and reproductive strategies. It sheds light on the hidden messages conveyed through displays of dominance, courtship rituals, and mate selection. By deciphering these messages, we gain a deeper appreciation for the evolutionary processes that have shaped the behaviors and interactions within species. We come to understand the delicate balance between competition and cooperation, the role of communication in mate selection, and the significance of reproductive success in the perpetuation of life.

Social hierarchies and mating rituals are integral components of animal behavior, serving as avenues for hidden messages to be communicated and received. They shape the dynamics within species, influence mate selection, and contribute to the continuation of life's intricate tapestry. Exploring the intricacies of social hierarchies and mating rituals offers a window into the evolutionary adaptations and strategies that have shaped the animal kingdom, enriching our understanding of the diverse and remarkable world of nature.

Hidden Messages in Landscapes

Natural Landforms as Symbols

The Earth's surface is a canvas upon which nature paints its magnificent landscapes, each landform telling a story of geological processes, environmental interactions, and cultural significance. Beyond their physical beauty, these natural landforms also hold profound symbolic meaning, offering a window into the hidden messages embedded in the fabric of the Earth itself.

Mountains, with their majestic peaks reaching towards the heavens, have long been revered as symbols of strength, endurance, and spiritual significance. They stand as symbols of resilience, challenging us to overcome obstacles and reach new heights. The towering presence of mountains often evokes a sense of awe and reverence, reminding us of our smallness in the face of nature's grandeur.

Rivers, meandering through landscapes with their graceful curves and flowing waters, are symbols of change, transformation, and the passage of time. They carry within them the ebb and flow of life, symbolizing the constant movement and evolution of nature. Rivers have played a crucial role in human history and mythology, serving as sources of sustenance, transportation, and spiritual inspiration. They symbolize the journey of life, as we navigate the currents and embrace the changes that come our way.

Caves, with their mysterious depths hidden beneath the Earth's surface, are symbols of the unknown, the subconscious, and hidden knowledge. These dark recesses have captivated human imagination for centuries, often associated with hidden treasures, spiritual retreats, and initiation rites. Exploring the depths of caves is like delving into the depths of our own souls, confronting the mysteries that lie within and uncovering hidden truths.

Deserts, vast and seemingly barren landscapes, are symbols of solitude, introspection, and resilience. In their arid expanses, life has found unique ways to adapt and survive, reminding us of the inherent strength and resilience within ourselves. Deserts also offer a sense of stillness and solitude, providing an opportunity for introspection and self-discovery. They invite us to embrace the quietude and listen to the whispers of our inner selves.

Coastlines, where land meets the sea, are symbols of transition, boundaries, and the interplay between two contrasting worlds. They represent the meeting point of stability and fluidity, offering a dynamic space where diverse ecosystems thrive. Coastlines symbolize the interconnectedness of land and sea, reminding us of the delicate balance and intricate relationships between different elements of nature.

Volcanoes, with their fiery eruptions and transformative power, are symbols of creation, destruction, and renewal. They embody the raw forces of nature, reminding us of the constant cycles of change and transformation. Volcanoes symbolize the potential for new beginnings that emerge from the ashes of destruction, inviting us to embrace the transformative power within ourselves.

These are just a few examples of how natural landforms carry symbolic meaning that transcends their physical attributes. They serve as powerful metaphors for aspects of the human experience, offering insights and reflections on our own journey through life. By attuning ourselves to the hidden messages encoded within natural landforms, we deepen our connection with the Earth and gain a greater appreciation for the profound wisdom and beauty that surrounds us.

Natural landforms are not only remarkable physical features of the Earth but also vessels of symbolism and hidden messages. Mountains, rivers, caves, deserts, coastlines, and volcanoes all carry profound meaning, inviting us to explore the depths of our own existence and connect with the larger tapestry of nature. By recognizing the symbolic significance of these landforms, we embark on a journey of discovery, unveiling the timeless wisdom that lies beneath the surface of the Earth's landscape.

Ancient Petroglyphs and Their Meaning

Carved into the surfaces of rocks, ancient petroglyphs stand as silent messengers from the past, preserving the wisdom, stories, and symbols of ancient civilizations. These intricate and mysterious markings hold a wealth of hidden messages, providing us with a glimpse into the beliefs, cultural practices, and artistic expressions of our ancestors.

Petroglyphs can be found across the globe, from remote desert canyons to rocky cliffs overlooking vast landscapes. They serve as a testament to the enduring human desire to communicate and leave a lasting mark on the world. Through the study and interpretation of these ancient carvings, we unravel the hidden messages embedded within the stone, shedding light on the diverse cultures and belief systems that have shaped our history.

The meanings of petroglyphs vary greatly, as they reflect the unique perspectives and experiences of different cultures. Some petroglyphs depict animals, capturing the essence and symbolism associated with these creatures. Animal motifs often represent qualities such as strength, wisdom, or spiritual significance, reflecting the reverence and close connection ancient cultures had with the natural world. These animal depictions may also convey stories, legends, or spiritual teachings passed down through generations.

Other petroglyphs depict human figures engaged in various activities, from hunting and gathering to ceremonial rituals. These figures offer glimpses into the daily lives, social structures, and cultural practices of ancient communities. They reveal the roles and responsibilities of different individuals within the society, as well as the significance of communal activities and spiritual beliefs.

Abstract symbols and geometric patterns are also common elements in petroglyphs. These intricate designs hold layers of meaning, often representing cosmological concepts, celestial bodies, or spiritual realms. The repetition of specific symbols or patterns across different petroglyph sites may indicate shared cultural or spiritual motifs, offering insights into the interconnectedness of ancient civilizations.

Petroglyphs also serve as a form of visual storytelling, conveying narratives and legends that have stood the test of time. They may depict scenes from creation myths, heroic tales, or significant events in the history of a particular culture. These stories provide glimpses into the collective memory of ancient societies, offering us a profound connection to our human heritage and the stories that have shaped us.

Deciphering the meaning of ancient petroglyphs requires a multidisciplinary approach, combining archaeological evidence, cultural context, and the insights of indigenous communities. It is a delicate and respectful process that recognizes the importance of cultural preservation and collaboration. The interpretation of petroglyphs must be approached with sensitivity, acknowledging the limitations of our understanding while valuing the knowledge and wisdom of the communities whose ancestors created these remarkable works of art.

Studying ancient petroglyphs not only enriches our understanding of the past but also fosters a deeper appreciation for the interconnectedness of humanity and the enduring power of symbolic communication. It invites us to reflect on our own connection to the natural world and the messages we choose to leave for future generations. Just as ancient civilizations expressed their beliefs and stories through petroglyphs, we too can find inspiration in the art of communication with nature, leaving our own messages of reverence, gratitude, and respect for the Earth.

Ancient petroglyphs hold a profound significance as repositories of hidden messages from the past. Through their intricate designs and symbols, they offer insights into the beliefs, stories, and cultural practices of ancient civilizations. Petroglyphs provide a bridge between our modern world and the wisdom of our ancestors, reminding us of the universal human desire to communicate, express, and preserve our collective heritage. Exploring the meaning of these ancient carvings unveils the rich tapestry of human history and fosters a deep sense of connection with the timeless beauty of the natural world.

The Art of Geomancy

Throughout history, humans have sought to understand and interpret the subtle energies and hidden messages embedded in the Earth itself. Geomancy, an ancient practice that spans cultures and continents, provides a pathway to uncovering these mystical connections between the physical and the spiritual realms. By studying the patterns, alignments, and energies of the natural world, geomancy offers insights into the profound interplay between the Earth and its inhabitants.

At its core, geomancy recognizes the Earth as a living entity, imbued with its own intelligence and energy. It acknowledges that the land we walk upon, the mountains that touch the sky, the rivers that flow, and the forests that teem with life are not mere physical entities but repositories of deeper wisdom and spiritual significance. Geomancy invites us to engage with the Earth as a sacred canvas upon which hidden messages are inscribed, waiting to be deciphered.

One of the key principles of geomancy is the understanding that the Earth possesses energetic lines and nodes, known as ley lines and power spots. These invisible pathways of energy crisscross the Earth's surface, connecting sacred sites, ancient landmarks, and natural formations. They form a complex web of interconnectedness, influencing the flow of energy and shaping the landscape in profound ways. Geomancers study and map these energetic pathways, recognizing their significance in the formation of sacred sites and the alignment of ancient structures.

The art of geomancy involves reading and interpreting the subtle energies present in the Earth's features. This includes studying the placement of mountains, the flow of water, the arrangement of trees, and the shape of the land itself. By attuning to these natural elements, geomancers gain insights into the energetic qualities of a place, unlocking the hidden messages encoded within its physical form. This deep understanding allows them to identify power spots, places of heightened energy and spiritual resonance, where individuals can connect more deeply with the Earth and its mysteries.

Geomancy is not limited to the external landscape; it also encompasses the energetic dynamics of the built environment. The placement and alignment of buildings, the arrangement of rooms, and the use of sacred geometry all play a role in creating harmonious and energetically balanced spaces. Geomancers work with these principles, seeking to create environments that are in harmony with the Earth's natural energies, fostering balance, vitality, and well-being.

Beyond the physical realm, geomancy recognizes the presence of subtle beings and spirits that inhabit the land. These unseen forces, often referred to as nature spirits or devas, are intimately connected with the Earth and its ecosystems. Geomancers understand the importance of honoring and working in collaboration with these beings, fostering a respectful and reciprocal relationship with the natural world. By acknowledging and respecting the presence of these unseen allies, geomancers tap into a deeper level of understanding and connection with the Earth's hidden messages.

Geomancy also encompasses the practice of dowsing, a technique used to detect and interact with subtle energies. Dowsers use tools such as divining rods or pendulums to locate underground water sources, ley lines, or other energetic phenomena. This ancient practice demonstrates the ability of humans to tap into the unseen forces that permeate the Earth, further highlighting the interconnectedness between ourselves and the natural world.

By embracing the art of geomancy, we develop a profound appreciation for the Earth's hidden messages and the intricate web of energies that shape our existence. It encourages us to see beyond the physical landscape and connect with the spiritual dimensions of our environment. Geomancy invites us to become stewards of the Earth, honoring and preserving its sacred sites, and cultivating a deep sense of harmony and balance within ourselves and our surroundings.

The art of geomancy unveils the hidden messages woven into the fabric of the Earth. It offers a pathway to understanding the energetic tapestry that connects us to the land, the natural world, and the unseen forces that shape our existence. Through the study of ley lines, power spots, sacred geometry, and the dynamics of the built environment, geomancy reveals the profound interplay between the physical and spiritual realms. By embracing this ancient practice, we deepen our connection with the Earth and gain insights that can guide us on a path of harmony, reverence, and co-creation with the natural world.

Unveiling Secrets through Nature's Cycles

The Symbolism of Seasons

Nature's cyclical rhythm unfolds through the ever-changing seasons, each bearing its own unique symbolism and hidden messages. The shifting landscapes and transformations that accompany the cycle of seasons have captivated humanity for millennia, inspiring awe, contemplation, and a deep connection to the natural world. In this chapter, we delve into the profound symbolism carried by the seasons, uncovering the wisdom and insights they offer.

Spring, the season of rebirth and renewal, holds a powerful symbolism of new beginnings. As winter's frost gives way to the gentle warmth of the sun, nature awakens from its slumber. The budding of flowers, the return of migratory birds, and the emergence of fresh greenery symbolize growth, fertility, and the cycle of life. Spring teaches us the beauty and resilience of transformation, inviting us to embrace change and harness the energy of renewal in our own lives.

Summer arrives in full bloom, bringing with it a vibrant burst of life and abundance. The sun shines brightly, nurturing the growth of crops, forests, and gardens. Summer symbolizes vitality, joy, and the peak of life's richness. It reminds us to bask in the warmth of the present moment, to savor the fruits of our labor, and to find delight in the simple pleasures that nature graciously provides. Summer teaches us to embrace the fullness of life and to express gratitude for the abundance that surrounds us.

Autumn, with its fiery colors and gentle descent, carries the symbolism of transition and letting go. As the days shorten and temperatures cool, the natural world undergoes a magnificent transformation. Trees shed their leaves in a magnificent display of reds, yellows, and oranges, reminding us of the beauty and impermanence of all things. Autumn invites us to release what no longer serves us, to shed the old and make way for new possibilities. It teaches us the art of surrender, urging us to trust in the cycles of life and find grace in the process of change.

Winter arrives, enveloping the land in a blanket of stillness and introspection. The trees stand bare, the earth rests beneath a layer of frost, and the world seems to slow down. Winter carries the symbolism of introspection, solitude, and inner growth. It is a time for reflection, for turning inward, and for nurturing the seeds of inspiration and creativity that lie dormant within us. Winter teaches us the value of silence and stillness, guiding us to embrace the wisdom that emerges from the depths of our being.

The symbolism of seasons extends beyond their individual characteristics. It also reflects the broader cycles of life, reminding us of the impermanence and interconnectedness of all things. The seasons mirror our own journeys, with their cycles of birth, growth, maturity, and eventual release. They teach us the importance of embracing the ebb and flow of life, of honoring the natural rhythms that govern our existence.

Moreover, the symbolism of seasons is woven into cultural and spiritual traditions worldwide. From the ancient rituals celebrating the equinoxes and solstices to the myths and folklore that narrate the changing seasons, humanity has long recognized and revered the profound messages carried by nature's cycles. These traditions remind us of our deep connection to the Earth and invite us to participate in the sacred dance of life.

By attuning ourselves to the symbolism of seasons, we gain a deeper understanding of our place within the natural world. We learn to live in harmony with the cycles of nature, honoring the lessons and messages they offer. The seasons invite us to embrace the ever-changing nature of our lives, to find beauty in each moment, and to celebrate the richness of our experiences.

The symbolism of seasons invites us to engage with the cyclical nature of life, to appreciate the transformative power of change, and to cultivate a profound connection with the natural world. As we immerse ourselves in the symbolism of seasons, we open ourselves to the hidden messages that nature offers, allowing them to guide and inspire us on our journey of self-discovery and growth.

Lunar and Solar Cycles

The celestial dance of the moon and the sun holds immense significance in the realm of hidden messages in nature. The rhythmic cycles of the lunar and solar bodies have guided human cultures and civilizations for centuries, providing insight, wisdom, and a deeper understanding of the natural world. In this chapter, we explore the profound symbolism and hidden messages embedded within the lunar and solar cycles.

The moon, with its gentle and mysterious glow, has long been regarded as a symbol of femininity, intuition, and emotional depth. Its waxing and waning phases mirror the ebb and flow of life, offering us a powerful metaphor for transformation and renewal. The new moon represents beginnings and fresh starts, a time to set intentions and plant the seeds of our desires. As the moon waxes and grows, it symbolizes expansion, abundance, and manifestation. Conversely, the waning moon invites us to release what no longer serves us, to let go of old patterns and beliefs that hinder our growth. By attuning ourselves to the lunar cycles, we gain a deeper understanding of our own inner rhythms and the cyclical nature of our emotions.

The solar cycle, marked by the rising and setting of the sun, holds its own unique symbolism and messages. The sun is a symbol of vitality, illumination, and life force energy. It represents our conscious awareness and the radiance of our true selves. The rising sun at dawn signifies new beginnings, the dawning of a fresh day filled with possibilities. It invites us to awaken to our fullest potential and to embrace the light within us. As the sun reaches its zenith at noon, it symbolizes strength, clarity, and the peak of our personal power. It encourages us to shine our light brightly and to express our authentic selves. And as the sun sets, casting a warm golden glow, it signifies closure and reflection, inviting us to review our day, to appreciate our accomplishments, and to find gratitude for the experiences that have shaped us. By attuning ourselves to the solar cycles, we align with the natural rhythms of energy and gain a deeper connection to the world around us.

The lunar and solar cycles also intersect and intertwine, creating powerful energetic dynamics. The phases of the moon are closely linked to the solar cycles, influencing tides, agricultural practices, and human behavior. The alignment of the new moon with the solar eclipse or the full moon with the lunar eclipse amplifies the energies and messages conveyed by both celestial bodies. These celestial events are often seen as potent opportunities for personal and collective transformation, calling us to harness the unique energies they offer.

Across cultures and traditions, lunar and solar cycles have been celebrated and honored through rituals, ceremonies, and festivals. From the solstices and equinoxes to the full moon gatherings and new moon rituals, humanity has recognized the profound influence of these celestial cycles on our lives. By engaging in these practices, we tap into the wisdom and energy that flow from the cosmos, deepening our connection to nature and the hidden messages it holds.

The lunar and solar cycles have been intricately woven into mythologies, folklore, and spiritual teachings. Stories of the moon goddesses and sun deities abound, symbolizing the cosmic forces at play and providing archetypal narratives that guide our understanding of the world. The moon's association with feminine energy and the sun's connection to masculine energy reflect the balance and harmony inherent in nature.

In conclusionTour existence. By embracing the hidden messages carried by the moon and the sun, we deepen our connection to the natural world, gain insights into our inner landscape, and align ourselves with the larger tapestry of life. The lunar and solar cycles serve as guides, illuminating our path, and reminding us that we are part of a greater cosmic dance. Through awareness and reverence for these cycles, we unlock the profound wisdom that nature offers and embark on a transformative journey of self-discovery.

Animal Migration and Seasonal Patterns

One of the most remarkable phenomena in the natural world is the migration of animals. Across vast distances and varied landscapes, countless species embark on extraordinary journeys, following ancient paths etched in their DNA. The intricate dance between animal migration and seasonal patterns reveals a tapestry of hidden messages and profound interconnectedness.

Migration is a testament to the resilience and adaptability of species. Birds, mammals, fish, and even insects undertake epic migrations, driven by the changing seasons and the pursuit of resources, breeding grounds, or favorable climates. These migrations span continents, traverse oceans, and often involve awe-inspiring feats of endurance and navigation.

The seasonal patterns play a crucial role in guiding and synchronizing these migrations. As the earth tilts on its axis, the shifting seasons bring about changes in temperature, daylight hours, and resource availability. Animals have finely tuned biological clocks that sense these changes, triggering instinctual behaviors and the start of their migration journeys.

Spring is a season of renewal and abundance. It is a time when migratory species begin their remarkable treks, often traveling thousands of miles to reach their breeding grounds. Birds embark on arduous flights, crossing borders and continents, guided by celestial cues and magnetic fields. Many species return faithfully to the same locations year after year, relying on hidden messages ingrained in their genetic code and imprinted in their ancestral memory.

Summer brings a flurry of activity as animals establish territories, build nests, and raise their young. It is a season of nurturing and growth, with ample food and resources available. Some species, like certain fish, undertake freshwater or marine migrations, seeking spawning grounds where their offspring will have the best chance of survival. These journeys are finely tuned to take advantage of favorable conditions and the abundance of food sources.

Autumn, with its vivid colors and crisp air, marks a time of transition. For many migratory species, it is a season of departure, as they prepare for long and often perilous journeys back to their wintering grounds. The hidden messages of instinct guide them on their way, ensuring they arrive at their destinations before the harsh winter sets in. Some species, such as monarch butterflies, embark on multi-generational migrations, with each generation passing down the knowledge of the route to the next.

Winter brings its own challenges, with cold temperatures and scarce resources. Many animals migrate to warmer regions or lower elevations, where they can find shelter and sustenance during the colder months. From whales navigating vast oceanic routes to ungulates traveling across snow-covered landscapes, the migration patterns in winter demonstrate the resilience and adaptability of these remarkable creatures.

The interplay between animal migration and seasonal patterns goes beyond mere survival and reproduction. It holds deeper symbolic significance. Animal migrations remind us of the cyclical nature of life, the impermanence of seasons, and the interconnectedness of all living beings. They invite us to recognize our own migratory nature, the ebb and flow of our experiences, and the importance of embarking on our own inner journeys of growth and transformation.

Animal migrations serve as ecological barometers, indicating the health and vitality of ecosystems. Disruptions to these patterns can have far-reaching consequences, affecting not only the migratory species but also the intricate web of life they are part of. By understanding and appreciating these hidden messages in nature, we can work towards conservation and stewardship, ensuring the preservation of these awe-inspiring migrations for future generations.

Animal migration and seasonal patterns unveil a world of hidden messages in nature. They embody the resilience, adaptability, and interconnectedness of species, guiding them on epic journeys across the globe. By observing and understanding these migrations, we gain a deeper appreciation for the cyclical nature of life, the profound interconnectedness of all living beings, and the urgent need to protect and preserve the delicate balance of our natural world.

Hidden Messages in Plants and Flowers

The Language of Flowers

In the enchanting world of nature, flowers hold a special place as messengers of beauty, emotion, and symbolism. Beyond their aesthetic appeal, flowers possess a language of their own, conveying hidden messages that have captivated cultures and civilizations throughout history. Delving into the language of flowers unveils a tapestry of meanings, sentiments, and connections that invite us to deepen our understanding of the natural world and ourselves.

The language of flowers, also known as floriography, traces its origins back to ancient times. In different cultures and traditions, specific flowers were assigned symbolic meanings, often associated with emotions, virtues, or events. These meanings were encoded in bouquets, floral arrangements, and even wearable flowers, allowing individuals to communicate unspoken sentiments and intentions.

Throughout history, flowers have been used as a means of expressing love, friendship, gratitude, and condolence. Each flower carries its own unique symbolism, infused with layers of cultural significance. For example, the rose, with its velvety petals and intoxicating fragrance, has long been associated with love and romance. The lotus, revered in many Eastern cultures, symbolizes purity, enlightenment, and spiritual awakening.

The language of flowers is not limited to individual species; it also encompasses the arrangement, color, and combination of flowers. The position of a flower in a bouquet or the choice of complementary blooms can convey nuanced meanings. A single red rose signifies passionate love, while a bouquet of mixed flowers can represent friendship, diversity, and the interconnectedness of different emotions.

Color plays a significant role in the language of flowers, as each hue carries its own symbolic connotations. Vibrant reds symbolize love and passion, while gentle pinks evoke feelings of tenderness and admiration. Yellow flowers convey joy and friendship, while white blooms symbolize purity, innocence, and remembrance. The language of flowers allows us to harness the power of color to express emotions and create meaningful connections.

Beyond their visual beauty and symbolic meanings, flowers also possess aromas that can evoke powerful memories and emotions. The scent of lavender can promote relaxation and tranquility, while the invigorating fragrance of citrus blossoms can uplift and energize. Flowers have the remarkable ability to engage our senses and transport us to different emotional states, connecting us to the natural world in profound ways.

In addition to their individual meanings, flowers also hold cultural and historical significance. They have been used in rituals, ceremonies, and celebrations, representing fertility, abundance, and renewal. From ancient civilizations to modern-day practices, flowers have adorned wedding ceremonies, religious rituals, and commemorative events, serving as vessels for hidden messages and expressions of collective sentiment.

The language of flowers transcends barriers of language and culture, providing a universal medium of communication and connection. It reminds us of the deep interplay between humans and nature, offering a profound reminder of our place in the natural world. By engaging with the language of flowers, we cultivate a deeper appreciation for the intricate beauty of nature, the power of symbolism, and the profound impact of even the smallest gestures.

The language of flowers is a captivating realm within nature's hidden messages. It invites us to explore the rich symbolism, meanings, and emotions that flowers convey. By understanding the language of flowers, we unlock a deeper connection with the natural world and discover new avenues for self-expression, appreciation, and connection with others. It is a language that speaks to the soul, allowing us to communicate and celebrate life's most profound experiences through the universal language of nature's blossoms.

Medicinal and Symbolic Properties of Plants

Plants have been our faithful companions since the dawn of human civilization, providing sustenance, shelter, and healing. Beyond their practical uses, plants hold a treasury of medicinal and symbolic properties that have shaped cultures and traditions around the world. Exploring the diverse world of plants opens a gateway to discovering their remarkable healing potential and the profound symbolism they carry.

For centuries, various cultures have recognized the medicinal properties of plants and harnessed their healing powers to treat ailments and restore balance within the body. Traditional systems of medicine, such as Ayurveda, Traditional Chinese Medicine, and Native American herbalism, have deep-rooted knowledge of the therapeutic qualities of plants. These systems have identified specific plants and their parts—leaves, flowers, roots, and bark—that possess potent medicinal compounds.

From the soothing properties of chamomile for calming nerves to the antimicrobial effects of garlic, plants offer a wide array of remedies for common ailments. Echinacea is renowned for its immune-boosting properties, while lavender is cherished for its ability to promote relaxation and improve sleep. The versatile aloe vera provides relief for burns and skin irritations, and turmeric has gained popularity for its anti-inflammatory benefits. Each plant carries its unique blend of chemical compounds that interact with our bodies in intricate ways, offering natural alternatives to conventional medicine.

However, while many plants offer therapeutic benefits, it is crucial to exercise caution and respect for their potential dangers. Some plants contain toxic substances that can be harmful or even fatal if consumed or improperly used. It is essential to educate ourselves about the potential risks associated with specific plants and consult reliable sources, such as botanists, herbalists, or reputable reference materials, to ensure safe usage.

The symbolic properties of plants go beyond their medicinal applications, intertwining with cultural and spiritual practices. Throughout history, plants have been imbued with symbolic meanings, representing virtues, emotions, and spiritual concepts. The lotus, revered in many Eastern cultures, symbolizes purity, enlightenment, and spiritual growth. The olive branch has come to represent peace and harmony, while the oak tree signifies strength, endurance, and wisdom.

Plants have also played a significant role in religious and ceremonial practices. Sacred plants, such as sage, cedar, and palo santo, are used in smudging rituals to cleanse and purify spaces, while incense made from resinous tree sap is burned as an offering to deities in various traditions. The holly plant, with its evergreen leaves and bright red berries, holds symbolic significance during winter festivities, symbolizing protection and renewal.

In addition to their medicinal and symbolic properties, plants contribute to the overall well-being of our environment. They play a vital role in maintaining ecological balance, acting as air purifiers, soil stabilizers, and habitats for diverse wildlife. By understanding the value of plants beyond their immediate benefits to humans, we develop a deeper appreciation for their intrinsic worth and the urgent need to protect and conserve our natural resources.

Plants possess both medicinal and symbolic properties that enrich our lives in profound ways. They offer a treasure trove of natural remedies, healing us physically and emotionally. Additionally, plants embody cultural, spiritual, and ecological significance, bridging the gap between humans and the natural world. It is essential to approach plants with respect, understanding their potential risks and harnessing their power responsibly. By embracing the medicinal and symbolic properties of plants, we embark on a journey of connection, harmony, and holistic well-being.

Plant Communication and Defense Mechanisms

While plants may appear static and silent, they possess a remarkable ability to communicate and defend themselves in the intricate web of the natural world. Hidden beneath their roots, leaves, and flowers lies a complex network of signals and responses, enabling plants to interact with their environment and protect themselves from threats. Exploring the fascinating realm of plant communication and defense mechanisms reveals a world of hidden messages and survival strategies.

Plants communicate with their surroundings through a variety of channels, employing chemical, acoustic, and visual signals. Through the release of volatile organic compounds, plants emit chemical signals that can attract beneficial organisms, repel pests, or warn nearby plants of impending danger. These chemical messages, known as allelochemicals, can influence the growth and behavior of neighboring plants, shaping the dynamics of plant communities.

Acoustic communication, though less widely known, also plays a role in plant interactions. Recent research has revealed that plants generate ultrasonic vibrations in response to environmental cues or stressors. These vibrations can serve as a form of communication, allowing plants to transmit information about potential threats or changing conditions to their neighboring companions.

In addition to chemical and acoustic signals, plants utilize visual cues as a means of communication. Brightly colored flowers and fruits attract pollinators, ensuring the continuation of their species through successful reproduction. Conversely, some plants have evolved warning signals, such as thorns or spines, to deter herbivores and protect their delicate tissues. These visual messages are essential in shaping plant-animal interactions and promoting survival.

Beyond communication, plants have developed an impressive array of defense mechanisms to protect themselves from various threats. For instance, some plants produce toxic compounds as a defense against herbivores. The alkaloids found in certain plants, such as foxgloves and poppies, act as potent chemical deterrents, making them unpalatable or even lethal to would-be grazers.

Another fascinating defense strategy employed by plants is the induction of physical barriers. In response to attack or injury, plants can reinforce their cell walls, produce additional layers of protective tissues, or even thicken their leaves and stems. These physical adaptations act as a shield, fortifying the plant against further damage and reducing the likelihood of successful herbivory.

Plants also have the ability to call for reinforcements when under attack. When a plant is damaged by an herbivore, it can release chemical signals that attract predators or parasitoids capable of preying on the attacking herbivores. This indirect defense mechanism, known as induced systemic resistance, exemplifies the sophisticated strategies plants employ to protect themselves.

Furthermore, plants exhibit remarkable resilience and adaptability in the face of environmental challenges. They can adjust their growth patterns, alter their metabolic processes, or even enter a state of dormancy to survive harsh conditions such as drought, extreme temperatures, or nutrient scarcity. Through these adaptive mechanisms, plants demonstrate their resilience and ability to thrive in diverse ecosystems.

Studying plant communication and defense mechanisms not only unveils the extraordinary strategies employed by these living organisms but also underscores the interconnectedness of the natural world. It highlights the complex web of relationships between plants, insects, animals, and even microorganisms, shaping the dynamics of entire ecosystems.

Plants possess a sophisticated repertoire of communication and defense mechanisms that enable them to interact with their environment and protect themselves from threats. Through chemical, acoustic, and visual signals, plants convey messages to neighboring organisms, shaping their growth and behavior. Their defense mechanisms, including toxic compounds, physical adaptations, and indirect defenses, showcase their resilience and survival strategies. By delving into the realm of plant communication and defense, we gain a deeper understanding of the hidden messages and intricate mechanisms that shape the natural world around us.

The Enigma of Symbiotic Relationships

Mutualism, Commensalism, and Parasitism

Within the intricate tapestry of nature, there exists a captivating phenomenon known as symbiosis – a delicate dance of interdependence between different organisms. Symbiotic relationships provide a fascinating glimpse into the hidden messages and intricate connections that shape the natural world. Among the various forms of symbiosis, three fundamental types stand out: mutualism, commensalism, and parasitism.

Mutualism represents a harmonious partnership in which both participating species benefit. In this symbiotic relationship, each organism provides something of value to the other, resulting in a mutual exchange of resources, protection, or services. Take, for example, the mutualistic relationship between flowering plants and their pollinators. The plants offer nectar as a reward, while the pollinators, such as bees or butterflies, inadvertently carry pollen from one flower to another, facilitating the plants' reproduction. Both parties gain advantages from this interaction – the plants receive efficient pollination, while the pollinators acquire nourishment. Mutualistic relationships can be found throughout nature, forging intricate bonds between organisms and contributing to the overall stability and resilience of ecosystems.

Commensalism, on the other hand, describes a symbiotic relationship where one organism benefits while the other remains unaffected. In this intriguing arrangement, the benefiting organism takes advantage of its partner's presence or activities without causing harm or providing any direct benefits in return. A classic example is the relationship between cattle and cattle egrets. As cattle graze, they disturb insects from the grass, providing an easy meal for the egrets. The cattle, however, are unaffected by the birds' presence. Similarly, certain epiphytic plants that grow on the branches of trees utilize them as a platform for better access to sunlight, moisture, and nutrients. The host tree, although unharmed, provides a support structure for the epiphytes. Commensal relationships offer an interesting glimpse into the complex web of interactions in nature, where one organism can thrive without impacting its partner significantly.

In contrast to mutualism and commensalism, parasitism represents a relationship in which one organism benefits at the expense of another. In this often unequal partnership, the parasite exploits its host, deriving nourishment, shelter, or other resources while causing harm or impairing the host's fitness. Parasites have evolved numerous adaptations to ensure their survival and reproduction, often displaying intricate strategies for finding, infecting, and exploiting hosts. Examples of parasitic relationships abound in nature, from blood-sucking ticks and fleas to the insidious tapeworms and parasitic wasps. These relationships remind us that hidden beneath the beauty and balance of the natural world, there exists a struggle for survival, where some organisms rely on others for their sustenance.

Understanding the intricacies of mutualism, commensalism, and parasitism not only reveals the hidden messages embedded within these relationships but also sheds light on the delicate balance of nature. Each type of symbiotic interaction plays a crucial role in shaping ecosystems, influencing population dynamics, and driving the evolution of species. The study of symbiotic relationships prompts us to recognize the interconnectedness of all living beings and appreciate the complex web of dependencies that sustain life on our planet.

Symbiotic relationships present a captivating tapestry of interdependence in nature. Mutualism showcases the benefits of cooperation and resource exchange, while commensalism reveals the subtle ways organisms can exploit their environment. Parasitism, though often unsettling, serves as a reminder of the intricate struggle for survival. By delving into the enigma of symbiotic relationships, we uncover the hidden messages and delicate connections that underpin the natural world, ultimately deepening our appreciation for the intricate balance and resilience of life.

Decoding Hidden Messages in Interactions

In the intricate tapestry of nature, interactions between organisms hold hidden messages, revealing a complex web of relationships and dependencies. From the grand scale of ecosystems to the microscopic realm of microorganisms, decoding these interactions unveils profound insights into the inner workings of the natural world.

Every interaction in nature carries a message, a story waiting to be deciphered. These messages are conveyed through various means, including chemical signals, behavioral cues, and physical adaptations. By observing and understanding these interactions, we can unravel the mysteries and secrets that lie beneath the surface.

One fascinating aspect of decoding hidden messages in interactions is the role of communication. Communication permeates the natural world, allowing organisms to convey information, establish hierarchies, coordinate activities, and even deceive or defend themselves. From the intricate songs of birds to the complex dance of honeybees, communication plays a vital role in shaping interactions and influencing the behavior of individuals and groups.

Within symbiotic relationships, decoding hidden messages becomes particularly intriguing. Mutualistic interactions, where both organisms benefit, often involve intricate signals and cues. For instance, the cooperative behavior between cleaner fish and larger fish reveals an intricate dance of trust and communication. The cleaner fish signal their willingness to remove parasites by displaying distinctive patterns or performing specific movements, while the larger fish communicate their acceptance and cooperation. These subtle exchanges underscore the importance of trust and communication in successful mutualistic partnerships.

Decoding hidden messages also sheds light on the dynamics of predator-prey interactions. Predators employ a range of strategies to capture their prey, while prey species have evolved defense mechanisms to evade detection or escape predation. These interactions involve a complex interplay of signals and adaptations, where the predator must decode the prey's behavior and the prey must decipher the predator's intentions. Whether it's the camouflage of a chameleon, the warning colors of a poisonous frog, or the intricate mimicry of a harmless insect, these interactions reveal the underlying messages of survival and adaptation.

Beyond individual interactions, decoding hidden messages in ecological networks provides a deeper understanding of the interconnectedness of species and the functioning of ecosystems. In food webs, for example, each interaction between predator and prey or herbivore and plant conveys a message about energy flow, population dynamics, and ecological balance. Changes in one interaction can have cascading effects throughout the entire network, highlighting the delicate web of dependencies and the hidden messages that drive ecological stability or disruption.

Decoding hidden messages in interactions also encompasses the study of coevolution and the arms race between species. As organisms adapt to each other's presence and behaviors, they engage in an ongoing dialogue that shapes their evolution. This constant interplay of adaptations, counter-adaptations, and evolutionary responses reflects a profound message of dynamic change and adaptation in the natural world.

Decoding hidden messages in interactions allows us to glimpse the underlying principles and patterns that govern the intricate dance of life. It reminds us that every interaction, no matter how small or seemingly insignificant, carries meaning and significance. By honing our observational skills, delving into the intricate cues and signals, and unraveling the mysteries of communication and adaptation, we gain a deeper appreciation for the complexity and interconnectedness of the natural world.

Decoding hidden messages in interactions provides a fascinating journey of discovery. From the delicate cues of mutualistic partnerships to the intricate dance of predator-prey interactions, each interaction carries a message that reveals the underlying principles of survival, adaptation, and interdependence. By deciphering these messages, we unlock the secrets of nature and gain a profound appreciation for the intricate tapestry of life's interactions.

The Role of Symbiosis in Ecosystems

Symbiosis, the intimate and often mutually beneficial relationship between different species, plays a crucial role in shaping and maintaining the balance of ecosystems. Within these intricate connections, organisms form alliances, exchange resources, and rely on one another for survival. The study of symbiosis unveils a fascinating world of cooperation, dependency, and ecological interdependence.

One of the primary roles of symbiosis in ecosystems is the facilitation of nutrient cycling. Certain symbiotic relationships, such as mutualistic associations between plants and fungi known as mycorrhizae, enhance the absorption of nutrients from the soil. The fungi extend their hyphae into the plant roots, forming a symbiotic network that increases the surface area for nutrient uptake. In return, the fungi receive carbohydrates from the plants. This mutually beneficial exchange not only promotes the growth and vitality of individual organisms but also contributes to the overall nutrient cycling and productivity of the ecosystem.

Symbiotic relationships also play a critical role in ecosystem resilience and adaptation. When faced with environmental challenges, organisms can form symbiotic partnerships to enhance their survival strategies. For instance, some corals form symbiotic relationships with photosynthetic algae called zooxanthellae. The corals provide shelter and nutrients to the algae, while the algae contribute to the corals' energy needs through photosynthesis. This partnership allows corals to thrive in nutrient-poor waters and creates the vibrant and diverse ecosystems of coral reefs. In this way, symbiosis acts as a mechanism for organisms to adapt and thrive in challenging environments.

Symbiotic interactions can also influence the structure and dynamics of communities within ecosystems. For example, the relationships between pollinators and flowering plants shape the composition and diversity of plant communities. Bees, butterflies, birds, and other pollinators rely on nectar and pollen as food sources, while plants depend on them for cross-pollination and reproduction. This interdependence results in intricate networks of relationships that influence species abundance, distribution, and coexistence within ecosystems.

Furthermore, symbiosis can regulate population dynamics and limit the dominance of certain species. In parasitic relationships, for instance, parasites depend on host organisms for resources, but excessive parasitism can harm or even kill the host. This creates a delicate balance where the presence of parasites regulates the population size and behavior of host species, preventing them from becoming overly abundant. Such interactions ensure the diversity and stability of ecosystems by preventing the dominance of a single species.

The role of symbiosis extends beyond individual organisms and impacts the functioning of entire ecosystems. In the case of mutualistic relationships between plants and pollinators or seed dispersers, symbiosis ensures the reproduction and dispersion of plant species, influencing the composition and structure of plant communities. Symbiotic interactions also contribute to the resilience of ecosystems by promoting biodiversity, enhancing nutrient cycling, and supporting the efficient use of resources.

However, it is important to note that not all symbiotic relationships are mutualistic. Some involve one organism benefiting at the expense of another, such as in parasitic or commensal relationships. While these interactions may seem one-sided, they still play a role in shaping ecosystems by influencing population dynamics and resource allocation.

Symbiosis is a fundamental force that shapes the structure, function, and resilience of ecosystems. Through mutualistic partnerships, symbiosis promotes nutrient cycling, enhances adaptation, and contributes to the diversity and stability of ecological communities. By understanding the intricate web of symbiotic relationships, we gain insights into the complex dynamics of ecosystems and the delicate balance of interdependence among species. Embracing and protecting these symbiotic relationships is crucial for the conservation and sustainability of our natural world.

Deciphering Weather Patterns

Weather as a Language

Nature has a language of its own, and one of the most powerful and expressive ways it communicates with us is through weather. The ever-changing patterns of the sky, the movement of clouds, the feel of the wind, and the behavior of animals and plants in response to weather all convey messages that, when understood, offer insights into the workings of the natural world and our place within it.

Weather is a dynamic and intricate system influenced by various factors such as temperature, humidity, air pressure, and wind patterns. It reflects the Earth's complex interactions with the atmosphere, the oceans, and the sun. By observing and interpreting weather patterns, we can begin to decipher the messages that nature is conveying.

One of the key aspects of weather as a language is its ability to reflect and convey emotions and moods. Think of the peacefulness of a calm, sunny day, the anticipation in the air before a thunderstorm, or the serenity of a misty morning. Weather can evoke feelings within us and set the tone for our experiences in nature.

Beyond emotions, weather patterns can provide valuable information about the larger environmental conditions and changes occurring in the natural world. For instance, sudden drops in air pressure and the darkening of the sky often precede an impending storm, alerting us to seek shelter. The intensity and direction of the wind can indicate weather systems moving across the landscape. By paying attention to these signals, we can prepare ourselves and adjust our activities accordingly.

Moreover, weather influences the behavior and patterns of plants and animals, offering further clues to its language. Birds soaring high in the sky before a rainstorm, the closing of flower petals as a storm approaches, or the scurrying of small creatures before a gust of wind—all of these are messages encoded in the actions of living beings. Animals and plants have evolved to respond to changes in weather as a means of survival, and by observing their behavior, we can gain insights into the imminent weather conditions and the delicate balance of nature.

Weather also holds cultural and symbolic significance in different societies and traditions around the world. Throughout history, humans have assigned meanings and interpretations to various weather phenomena. Rain, for example, is often associated with renewal, cleansing, and fertility in many cultures. Snow can evoke a sense of purity and transformation. By exploring the cultural interpretations of weather, we gain a deeper appreciation of the diverse ways in which humans have sought to understand and connect with the natural world.

Understanding weather as a language requires patience, observation, and a willingness to engage with the natural environment. It invites us to slow down, to be present, and to attune our senses to the subtle shifts and rhythms of the atmosphere. By cultivating a deeper awareness of weather patterns and their meanings, we can develop a more profound connection with nature and tap into its wisdom.

Reading Cloud Formations

Clouds, floating high above us in an ever-changing display, hold a wealth of hidden messages waiting to be deciphered. These ethereal formations, formed by the condensation of water vapor in the atmosphere, offer a fascinating glimpse into the dynamics of weather and provide valuable insights into the language of nature.

Clouds come in a myriad of shapes, sizes, and textures, each with its own story to tell. By studying their formations, we can gain a deeper understanding of the current and future weather conditions, as well as the moods and energies present in the natural world. Clouds serve as a canvas upon which nature paints its messages, inviting us to become attentive observers and skilled interpreters.

One of the key aspects of reading cloud formations is recognizing their different types. Cumulus clouds, with their puffy, cotton-ball-like appearance, often indicate fair weather and a tranquil atmosphere. These clouds, scattered across the sky, evoke a sense of calm and serenity. On the other hand, towering cumulonimbus clouds, with their dark, ominous appearance, signify the potential for thunderstorms and intense downpours. They serve as nature's warnings, urging us to seek shelter and brace for the power of the elements.

Stratus clouds, with their uniform, layered structure, often bring overcast conditions and a sense of stillness. They can create a moody atmosphere and cast a mysterious aura over the landscape. Stratocumulus clouds, characterized by their low, lumpy formations, suggest a mixture of fair and unsettled weather, with the possibility of light rain showers. Observing these various cloud types allows us to gather clues about the current atmospheric conditions and make predictions about what lies ahead.

Furthermore, the texture and appearance of clouds offer additional insights into the language of nature. Wispy cirrus clouds, high in the sky, resemble delicate brushstrokes and often indicate the presence of moisture in the upper atmosphere. Their feathery appearance evokes a sense of lightness and grace. Cirrostratus clouds, thin and translucent, can create a veil-like covering across the sky, diffusing sunlight and creating halos around the sun or moon. These clouds hint at the possibility of impending weather changes.

As we learn to read cloud formations, it is essential to pay attention to their movements and transformations. Clouds are never static; they shift, merge, and dissipate, revealing the ever-changing dynamics of the atmosphere. The movement of clouds can indicate the direction and strength of the wind, providing insights into weather systems approaching or departing. Watching how clouds evolve over time allows us to witness the unfolding story of weather and its effects on the natural world.

Clouds also offer a space for imagination and reflection. Their shapes, resembling familiar objects or animals, invite us to tap into our creativity and find personal meaning within their fleeting forms. These cloud "pictures" spark our curiosity and encourage us to engage with nature in a playful and imaginative way.

Animal and Plant Behavior as Weather Indicators

In the intricate dance of nature, animals and plants possess a remarkable ability to sense and respond to changes in weather conditions. Their behavior becomes a valuable guide for those who seek to uncover the hidden messages embedded within the natural world. By observing the subtle cues and adaptations exhibited by these living beings, we can unravel the secrets of impending weather patterns and gain insights into the delicate balance between organisms and their environment.

Animals, with their finely tuned instincts, exhibit a range of behaviors that serve as reliable indicators of changing weather. Birds, for instance, display remarkable migratory patterns in response to shifting seasons. Their long-distance journeys reflect a deep connection to the rhythms of nature and a keen awareness of changing weather patterns. By observing the timing and direction of bird migrations, we can anticipate the arrival of different seasons and prepare ourselves for the shifts that lie ahead.

Furthermore, the behavior of animals such as insects, mammals, and marine creatures provides important clues about impending weather changes. For example, certain insects, like ants, become particularly active and frenzied in the hours preceding a rainstorm. Their heightened activity suggests a sensitivity to changes in atmospheric pressure and humidity. Similarly, some mammals, such as cows and horses, seek shelter or display restlessness before the onset of inclement weather. These observable changes in behavior offer valuable insights into the imminent weather conditions.

Plants, too, possess a language of their own, revealing weather patterns through their growth, flowering, and leaf behavior. The opening and closing of flowers throughout the day, known as nyctinasty, can be influenced by changes in temperature, humidity, and light levels. Additionally, the position of leaves, such as their orientation towards or away from the sun, can provide indications of impending rain or storms. By paying attention to these subtle plant behaviors, we can decipher the messages nature conveys about forthcoming weather events.

In addition to their immediate responses to changing weather conditions, both animals and plants exhibit long-term adaptations that reflect their ability to thrive in specific climates. For instance, the presence of certain plant species in a particular region can indicate the prevailing climate and soil conditions. The distribution of specific animal species, such as the presence of cold-weather adapted animals in polar regions, offers insights into the extreme environmental conditions found there. These adaptations highlight the intricate relationship between organisms and their environment, serving as a testament to nature's resilience and its ability to adapt to prevailing weather patterns.

By developing our observational skills and attuning ourselves to the behavior of animals and plants, we can become proficient interpreters of nature's weather messages. The insights gained from these observations enable us to prepare for changing weather conditions, make informed decisions about outdoor activities, and deepen our connection with the natural world. As we learn to recognize the subtle nuances of animal and plant behavior, we unlock a treasure trove of wisdom and understanding that transcends human language and taps into the profound interconnectedness of all living beings.

Enhancing Your Nature Connection

Cultivating Mindfulness in Nature

In today's fast-paced and technology-driven world, finding moments of peace and connection with nature has become more important than ever. As we immerse ourselves in the natural world, we have the opportunity to slow down, quiet our minds, and cultivate a sense of mindfulness. Mindfulness in nature allows us to fully engage with our surroundings, heightening our senses and deepening our connection with the hidden messages that nature holds.

Mindfulness is the practice of intentionally focusing our attention on the present moment and fully experiencing it without judgment. When we apply this practice to our interactions with nature, we open ourselves to a world of sensory wonders and profound insights. By becoming aware of our surroundings and grounding ourselves in the present, we can truly appreciate the beauty and intricacy of the natural world.

One of the key aspects of cultivating mindfulness in nature is developing a deep awareness of our senses. As we venture into natural spaces, we can pay close attention to the sights, sounds, smells, textures, and tastes that surround us. We might notice the gentle rustling of leaves, the vibrant colors of wildflowers, the sweet fragrance of blooming trees, or the soft touch of moss beneath our fingertips. By fully immersing ourselves in these sensory experiences, we awaken our senses and bring ourselves into the present moment.

Mindfulness in nature also involves embracing a sense of curiosity and wonder. As we observe the intricate details of plants, animals, and landscapes, we can approach them with a childlike fascination. Every leaf, every rock, and every creature becomes a source of discovery and amazement. We may find hidden patterns in the petals of a flower, witness the dance of sunlight filtering through the forest canopy, or marvel at the precision of a spider's web. Cultivating curiosity allows us to see beyond the surface and uncover the hidden messages that nature presents.

Furthermore, practicing mindfulness in nature encourages us to let go of distractions and mental chatter. We can release the stress and worries of everyday life and focus solely on the present moment. This requires us to quiet our minds and embrace stillness. As we sit in contemplation, we may find ourselves attuned to the gentle rhythm of nature—the soothing whispers of the wind, the steady flow of a nearby stream, or the rhythmic chirping of birds. In this stillness, we create space for reflection, introspection, and a deeper connection with our inner selves.

Mindfulness in nature also invites us to recognize our interconnectedness with all living beings. As we observe the intricate web of relationships and dependencies in ecosystems, we realize that we are an integral part of this grand tapestry of life. The delicate balance between plants, animals, and their environment becomes apparent, and we begin to appreciate our role as stewards of the natural world. This understanding fosters a sense of reverence and responsibility towards the Earth and all its inhabitants.

By cultivating mindfulness in nature, we embark on a transformative journey of self-discovery and connection. We learn to slow down, savor the present moment, and attune ourselves to the hidden messages that nature whispers. Mindfulness allows us to become active participants in the natural world, rather than mere observers. It deepens our relationship with the Earth and fosters a sense of gratitude, awe, and respect.

Nature Meditation and Deepening Awareness

Meditation is a powerful practice that allows us to cultivate inner stillness, clarity, and a deeper connection with ourselves and the world around us. When combined with the serenity and beauty of nature, meditation becomes an even more profound and transformative experience. Nature meditation enables us to tap into the wisdom of the natural world, deepen our awareness, and uncover hidden messages that can guide and inspire us.

To engage in nature meditation, find a quiet and peaceful spot in nature where you feel comfortable and undisturbed. It could be a secluded corner of a park, a serene forest clearing, a tranquil beach, or any natural setting that resonates with you. Sit comfortably, either cross-legged on the ground or on a cushion, with your back straight and relaxed. Close your eyes or soften your gaze, and take a few deep breaths to settle into the present moment.

As you begin your meditation, bring your attention to the sensations of your body. Feel the contact between your body and the earth beneath you. Notice the support and grounding that nature provides. Allow any tension or stress to melt away, releasing it into the earth with each exhale. Feel a sense of relaxation and connection with the natural environment.

Now, shift your awareness to the sounds around you. Listen attentively to the symphony of nature—the rustling of leaves, the chirping of birds, the gentle lapping of water, or the distant whisper of the wind. Observe these sounds without judgment or analysis, simply allowing them to be part of your meditation. Notice how they rise and fall, intertwining with the stillness within you.

Next, open your senses to the fragrances that fill the air. Inhale deeply and appreciate the subtle scents of flowers, trees, and earth. Let these aromas awaken your sense of smell and create a deeper connection with the natural world. Breathe in the vitality and life force that permeate the surroundings.

Now, gently bring your attention to the sensations on your skin. Feel the caress of a gentle breeze, the warmth of the sunlight, or the coolness of the shade. Allow your body to merge with the elements of nature, sensing the interconnectedness between yourself and the environment. Embrace the touch of nature as a reminder of your place within the intricate web of life.

As your body relaxes and your senses awaken, turn your attention inward. Notice the thoughts and emotions that arise within you. Rather than engaging with them or judging them, observe them as passing clouds in the sky of your awareness. Allow them to come and go, without attachment or resistance. Witness the ebb and flow of your inner landscape, mirroring the cycles of nature.

As you deepen your awareness, let your focus expand to encompass the broader environment. Observe the natural elements around you—the trees, plants, and animals. Notice their forms, movements, and interactions. See how they harmoniously coexist, each playing a unique role in the tapestry of life. Allow yourself to merge with this interconnectedness, recognizing that you are an integral part of this vast ecosystem.

In this state of expanded awareness, you may start to perceive hidden messages and wisdom that nature holds. Patterns, synchronicities, and subtle cues become more apparent. You may notice how the behavior of animals reflects the rhythms of nature, how the growth patterns of plants symbolize resilience and adaptability, or how the changing seasons mirror the cycles of life and transformation.

As you conclude your nature meditation, take a moment to express gratitude for the experience and the insights you have received. Reflect on how this practice has deepened your connection with the natural world and expanded your awareness. Carry this sense of mindfulness and connection with you as you navigate your daily life, allowing it to guide your actions and decisions.

Nature meditation is a powerful tool for deepening our awareness and accessing the hidden messages that nature offers. By immersing ourselves in the beauty and serenity of the natural world, we open ourselves to profound insights and a heightened sense of interconnectedness. Through this practice, we can cultivate a more mindful and conscious relationship with nature, recognizing that we are not separate from it, but an integral part of its intricate tapestry.

Nature Rituals and Celebrations

Throughout human history, cultures around the world have recognized the sacredness and profound influence of nature in their lives. They have developed rituals and celebrations that honor and express gratitude for the gifts and messages that nature bestows upon us. These nature-based rituals serve as a bridge between the human and natural realms, allowing us to deepen our connection with the Earth and its inhabitants.

Nature rituals can take many forms, from simple daily practices to elaborate ceremonial events. They provide a space for us to commune with nature, express our reverence, and engage in transformative experiences. These rituals remind us of our inherent connection with the natural world and the wisdom it holds.

One common nature ritual is the act of greeting the sunrise or bidding farewell to the sunset. These rituals symbolize our connection to the cycles of day and night, reminding us of the perpetual rhythm of life. By witnessing these celestial events, we acknowledge the beauty and power of nature and set our intentions for the day or express gratitude for the day that has passed.

Another nature ritual is the practice of walking barefoot on the earth, also known as earthing or grounding. By removing the barriers between our feet and the earth's surface, we directly connect with the energy and vitality of the natural world. This ritual allows us to release any accumulated tension or stress and absorb the healing energy of the earth. It is a way of reconnecting with our roots and finding balance and stability.

In some cultures, the changing of the seasons is marked with elaborate rituals and celebrations. These ceremonies honor the transitions and cycles of nature and invite us to align our lives with these natural rhythms. For example, the spring equinox may be celebrated as a time of renewal and new beginnings, while the autumn equinox may be observed as a time of gratitude and reflection. These rituals serve as reminders to attune ourselves to the larger cycles of the Earth and to live in harmony with its changing seasons.

Nature rituals can also involve creating sacred spaces in nature, such as building altars or dedicating areas for prayer or meditation. These spaces act as focal points for our intentions and allow us to infuse the natural environment with our spiritual presence. By consciously arranging natural elements, such as stones, flowers, or leaves, we create a tangible representation of our connection with the Earth and the divine.

Additionally, nature-based celebrations often revolve around the harvest or the abundance of the natural world. These festivals serve as occasions to honor the interconnectedness of all living beings and express gratitude for the sustenance and resources that nature provides. Whether it's a harvest festival, a blessing of the fields, or a ceremony to honor a specific plant or animal, these celebrations connect us to the cycles of growth, nourishment, and reciprocity that exist in nature.

Nature rituals and celebrations remind us of our place within the intricate web of life. They invite us to slow down, to be present, and to attune ourselves to the wisdom and messages that nature offers. Through these rituals, we cultivate a deeper appreciation for the Earth, its ecosystems, and the delicate balance that sustains all living beings.

Incorporating nature rituals and celebrations into our lives can be a powerful way to honor and deepen our relationship with the natural world. These practices allow us to tap into the ancient wisdom and hidden messages that nature holds, fostering a sense of reverence, gratitude, and interconnectedness. As we engage in these rituals, we remember that we are not separate observers of nature, but active participants in its intricate dance. By aligning ourselves with the rhythms of nature, we find a sense of belonging and harmony that enriches our lives and the world around us.

Ethical Considerations in Nature Interpretation

Respecting Wildlife and Habitats

One of the fundamental principles of connecting with nature and finding hidden messages is the importance of respecting wildlife and their habitats. As we explore and immerse ourselves in natural environments, it is crucial that we approach them with a deep reverence for the delicate balance of ecosystems and the well-being of the creatures that inhabit them.

Respecting wildlife means recognizing their intrinsic value and understanding that they have their own lives, needs, and roles within the larger web of life. It involves refraining from actions that may harm or disrupt their natural behavior, and instead observing and appreciating them from a respectful distance.

First and foremost, it is vital to remember that we are visitors in the homes of wildlife. Their habitats are their sanctuaries, providing shelter, food, and breeding grounds. When we venture into these spaces, we must do so with a sense of humility and the understanding that we are entering their domain. By approaching wildlife with respect, we allow them to go about their lives undisturbed, maintaining the balance of their ecosystems.

One of the key aspects of respecting wildlife is avoiding any form of harassment or interference. This includes refraining from chasing, capturing, or touching animals. It is crucial to remember that wild animals are not domesticated pets. They rely on their instincts and natural behaviors for survival, and any disruption to these patterns can have detrimental effects on their well-being.

Furthermore, it is essential to be mindful of our impact on wildlife habitats. This means avoiding activities that can damage or degrade their environments. For example, staying on designated trails when hiking or exploring ensures that we minimize our footprint and avoid disturbing sensitive habitats. Additionally, we must be cautious when disposing of waste, as litter can harm wildlife and pollute their habitats.

Respecting wildlife also extends to refraining from feeding or approaching animals for the sake of entertainment or personal gain. Feeding wild animals can disrupt their natural foraging habits and make them dependent on human-provided food, which can lead to imbalances within the ecosystem. It is crucial to let animals find their own food sources and maintain their natural behaviors.

Another essential aspect of respecting wildlife and their habitats is understanding and abiding by local regulations and conservation efforts. Many areas have specific guidelines in place to protect wildlife, such as designated wildlife reserves, protected areas, or restricted access during certain seasons. By familiarizing ourselves with these regulations and following them diligently, we contribute to the preservation of natural habitats and the well-being of the animals that call them home.

Respecting wildlife and habitats is not only about the individual actions we take but also about fostering a mindset of empathy and responsibility towards the natural world. It involves cultivating an understanding of the interconnectedness of all living beings and recognizing our role as stewards of the Earth.

By respecting wildlife and their habitats, we create a harmonious coexistence between humans and nature. We allow wildlife to thrive undisturbed, ensuring the continuation of their vital roles in maintaining healthy ecosystems. Additionally, when we approach nature with respect, we open ourselves up to deeper connections and a greater understanding of the hidden messages that nature reveals to us.

Respecting wildlife and habitats is a lifelong commitment that requires continuous learning and growth. As we expand our knowledge and deepen our connection with the natural world, we become advocates for its protection and preservation. By instilling a sense of respect for wildlife in ourselves and future generations, we contribute to a more sustainable and harmonious relationship between humans and the natural world.

Responsible Nature Photography and Documenting

Photography has the incredible power to capture the beauty and intricacies of nature, allowing us to share and preserve moments that may otherwise be fleeting. It is a medium through which we can tell stories, evoke emotions, and inspire a deeper connection with the natural world. However, with this power comes great responsibility.

Responsible nature photography goes beyond capturing stunning images. It involves approaching the act of documenting nature with respect, mindfulness, and a commitment to the well-being of the subjects and their habitats. It is about being conscious of the impact we have as photographers and taking steps to ensure that our actions do not harm or disturb the very subjects we aim to celebrate.

One of the primary principles of responsible nature photography is to prioritize the welfare of the wildlife and their habitats. It means observing and photographing animals from a safe and respectful distance, using telephoto lenses or binoculars to capture intimate moments without intruding on their natural behavior. By giving animals the space they need to go about their lives undisturbed, we protect their well-being and preserve the integrity of their habitats.

Additionally, responsible nature photography involves being mindful of the environment in which we operate. This includes staying on designated trails or paths to avoid trampling delicate vegetation or disturbing nesting grounds. It means refraining from moving or manipulating natural elements to achieve a desired composition. The goal is to document nature as it is, without causing any harm or altering the natural balance of the scene.

Another crucial aspect of responsible nature photography is respecting the rules and regulations set forth by conservation organizations and local authorities. Many protected areas have specific guidelines in place to safeguard wildlife and their habitats. As responsible photographers, it is our duty to familiarize ourselves with these rules and adhere to them diligently. This may include obtaining permits, respecting restricted areas, or abiding by specific time restrictions to minimize our impact.

In the age of digital photography and social media, responsible nature photographers also have a role to play in promoting ethical practices online. This involves being transparent about our methods and ensuring that the captions and descriptions accompanying our images are accurate and informative. It means refraining from using editing techniques that misrepresent the natural scene or enhance the behavior of the wildlife. By maintaining honesty and integrity in our documentation, we contribute to a more authentic and respectful representation of the natural world.

Responsible nature photography extends beyond our actions in the field. It also encompasses the way we share and distribute our images. It is important to obtain consent and respect the privacy of individuals or communities featured in our photographs, especially in the case of indigenous cultures or sensitive locations. It means seeking permission when using images for commercial purposes and giving proper credit to the subjects and their habitats.

As nature photographers, we have the unique opportunity to not only document but also raise awareness about conservation issues and the importance of protecting our natural world. Through our images, we can tell stories that evoke empathy, inspire action, and celebrate the wonders of nature. By aligning our photography with responsible practices, we become advocates for the preservation of the environments and species we encounter.

Responsible nature photography is about more than capturing beautiful images. It is about fostering a deep respect for wildlife and their habitats, being mindful of our impact, and adhering to ethical principles in our documentation and sharing. By practicing responsible photography, we become storytellers and ambassadors for the natural world, inspiring others to cherish and protect the hidden messages that nature reveals to us through our lens.

Balancing Interpretation and Preservation

As we delve into the realm of deciphering hidden messages in nature, it is crucial to strike a delicate balance between interpretation and preservation. While our quest to unravel the secrets and symbolism embedded in the natural world is exciting and enlightening, we must always remember our responsibility to protect and preserve the very environments and creatures that inspire us.

Interpretation is the lens through which we view and understand nature's hidden messages. It involves drawing connections, discerning patterns, and unraveling the meanings that lie beneath the surface. Interpretation enables us to appreciate the intricacies and complexities of the natural world, offering insights into its profound wisdom and interconnectedness.

However, interpretation must be approached with humility and respect. It is essential to acknowledge that our understanding is often limited, and nature's mysteries are vast and ever-evolving. As we interpret the symbols and messages we encounter, we must remain open to new perspectives and be willing to revise our interpretations in light of new knowledge and discoveries.

Preservation, on the other hand, is the bedrock of our responsibility as stewards of the natural world. It involves safeguarding ecosystems, conserving biodiversity, and ensuring the sustainable use of natural resources. Preservation is not just about protecting the physical environment but also about nurturing the delicate balance of ecological relationships and respecting the inherent value of every living being.

The challenge lies in finding harmony between interpretation and preservation. It is not enough to simply interpret and appreciate the hidden messages in nature; we must actively work to protect the environments and organisms that give rise to these messages. Our interpretations should not be detached from the realities of conservation and sustainability.

One way to strike this balance is through education and awareness. By fostering a deeper understanding of the interconnections between nature's hidden messages and the need for preservation, we empower individuals to become informed and compassionate advocates for the natural world. Education can inspire a sense of responsibility and a desire to take action to protect the environments that hold these hidden messages.

Furthermore, interpretation and preservation can inform and support each other. As we interpret the messages in nature, we gain insights into the delicate web of life and the interconnectedness of all living beings. This understanding can fuel our passion for preservation, motivating us to work towards sustainable practices and conservation efforts that uphold the integrity of the natural world.

In practical terms, balancing interpretation and preservation requires us to approach nature with a mindset of reverence and mindfulness. It means treading lightly, leaving no trace of our presence, and minimizing our impact on the delicate ecosystems we explore. It means supporting and engaging with organizations and initiatives that champion conservation efforts and sustainable practices.

The harmony between interpretation and preservation lies in recognizing the intrinsic value of nature beyond its symbolism and hidden messages. It is about embracing the awe-inspiring beauty of the natural world and recognizing that it exists not just for our interpretation, but for its own sake. By valuing and preserving nature in its entirety, we ensure that future generations can continue to seek and decipher the hidden messages it holds.

Balancing interpretation and preservation is a vital aspect of our journey to uncover hidden messages in nature. By approaching interpretation with humility and respect, and by actively working to preserve and protect the environments that inspire us, we can create a harmonious relationship between our understanding and our responsibility as custodians of the natural world. In this delicate balance, we discover a profound connection to nature's hidden wisdom, while also ensuring its longevity and vitality for generations to come.

Conclusion

Continuing the Journey of Discovery

The journey of discovering hidden messages in nature is one that knows no bounds. It is a journey that transcends the pages of this book and extends into the vast expanse of the natural world. As we reach the end of this exploration, we find ourselves standing at the threshold of an infinite realm of possibilities, where new revelations and insights eagerly await our curious minds.

Continuing the journey of discovery means embracing a lifelong commitment to deepening our understanding of nature's hidden messages. It requires us to cultivate a sense of wonder and curiosity, to remain open to the mysteries that surround us, and to approach every encounter with the natural world as an opportunity for learning and growth.

One of the keys to continuing this journey is to nurture our observational skills. Nature has an endless array of patterns, phenomena, and interactions to offer, and by honing our ability to observe, we unlock a world of hidden meanings and connections. By sharpening our senses and immersing ourselves in the present moment, we become attuned to the subtle cues and intricate details that often go unnoticed. In the delicate dance of a butterfly, the rhythmic chirping of insects, or the gentle sway of a tree, there is a wealth of knowledge waiting to be unraveled.

Another crucial aspect of continuing the journey is to remain open to different perspectives and interpretations. Nature speaks in a language that transcends cultural boundaries and individual biases. By exploring the cultural interpretations of natural symbols, we gain a broader understanding of the rich tapestry of meanings that humans have attributed to the natural world throughout history. This opens our minds to new possibilities and deepens our appreciation for the diverse ways in which nature communicates its hidden messages.

Technology can also be a valuable tool on our journey. With advancements in photography, sound recording, and data collection, we have unprecedented opportunities to document and study the intricate nuances of nature. Through responsible nature photography and scientific research, we can capture the fleeting moments, the elusive behaviors, and the mesmerizing beauty that nature presents. These records not only serve as personal keepsakes but also contribute to our collective knowledge and understanding of the natural world.

As we venture further into the journey, we must also cultivate a deep sense of respect and reverence for the natural world. We must recognize that we are but one thread in the intricate tapestry of life, and our actions have consequences that ripple through the interconnected web of ecosystems. By practicing responsible and sustainable behaviors, by preserving habitats and protecting biodiversity, we become active participants in the delicate balance of nature.

The journey of discovery is not without its challenges. It requires patience, perseverance, and a willingness to embrace uncertainty. There will be times when the hidden messages elude us, when nature's secrets remain veiled. Yet, it is precisely in those moments of humility and awe that we are reminded of the vastness and complexity of the natural world. It is through these encounters with the unknown that our sense of wonder is reignited, inspiring us to continue seeking, questioning, and exploring.

In our quest to uncover nature's hidden messages, let us never forget the profound joy and fulfillment that this journey brings. It is a journey that nourishes our souls, expands our consciousness, and deepens our connection to the Earth. With each step we take, we become more attuned to the rhythms of nature, more aligned with its wisdom, and more committed to its preservation.

So, let us embark on this continuing journey of discovery with open hearts and minds. Let us embrace the beauty, the mystery, and the hidden messages that nature offers. And may this journey not only enrich our lives but also inspire us to become passionate advocates for the protection and conservation of our planet. For in our pursuit of hidden messages, we discover our own place in the intricate tapestry of life, and we become custodians of nature's most precious gifts.

Embracing Nature's Hidden Messages

In our exploration of nature's hidden messages, we have led a remarkable journey of discovery and wonder. Throughout these pages, we have delved into the symbolism, patterns, and language that permeate the natural world, revealing profound insights and connections that invite us to see beyond the surface and deepen our relationship with nature.

Embracing nature's hidden messages is an invitation to embrace a richer, more expansive understanding of the world around us. It is an acknowledgment that nature is not merely a backdrop or a resource for our use but a vibrant tapestry of wisdom, secrets, and stories waiting to be deciphered. As we open ourselves to this deeper level of engagement, we discover that every leaf, every animal, and every landscape carries whispers of meaning and significance.

In this journey, we have witnessed how nature holds clues, how symbolism weaves through its fabric, and how the language of animals and plants communicates profound truths. We have marveled at the intricate beauty of geometric patterns and the role of sacred geometry in natural forms. We have recognized the importance of observing, noticing patterns, and connecting the dots to uncover hidden messages.

We have explored the significance of colors, their cultural interpretations, and their role in conveying messages in the natural world. We have learned to decode the messages embedded in ancient petroglyphs, the art of geomancy, and the symbolism of seasons, lunar and solar cycles. We have witnessed the interplay of mutualism, commensalism, and parasitism, and the enigmatic web of symbiotic relationships.

Nature has revealed its language through weather patterns, cloud formations, and the behavior of animals and plants as indicators of environmental changes. We have cultivated mindfulness, engaged in nature meditation, and deepened our awareness of the profound interconnectedness of all life forms. We have embraced nature rituals and celebrations, and in doing so, reconnected with ancient traditions and the rhythm of the natural world.

As we conclude this exploration, it is important to recognize the immense responsibility that comes with unraveling nature's hidden messages. We must approach our interactions with nature with respect, reverence, and a commitment to preservation. By striking a balance between interpretation and preservation, we ensure that our journey of understanding does not disrupt the delicate ecosystems and the fragile habitats that provide us with such profound insights.

Embracing nature's hidden messages is an ongoing process, an ever-unfolding tapestry of discovery and connection. It invites us to be humble in the face of nature's vastness, to listen attentively to its whispers, and to cultivate a deep sense of wonder and awe. It is an invitation to forge a harmonious relationship with the natural world, where our interpretation is guided by preservation and our preservation is informed by interpretation.

As we embrace nature's hidden messages, we tap into a wellspring of wisdom, inspiration, and harmony. We discover that the language of nature is not separate from us but an integral part of our own existence. It speaks to our deepest longings, our innate curiosity, and our yearning for connection. It reminds us of our place in the intricate web of life and invites us to be mindful stewards of this precious planet we call home.

May this journey into the realm of hidden messages in nature serve as a catalyst for a lifelong exploration, a source of inspiration and contemplation, and a reminder of the boundless wonders that surround us. May it foster a deeper sense of reverence for the natural world and a commitment to its preservation. And may it ignite a spark within each of us to embark on our own unique quest to uncover the profound truths and hidden messages that nature so generously offers.

Printed in Great Britain
by Amazon